How to Teach

PRACTICAL GUIDES FOR LIBRARIANS

About the Series

This innovative series written and edited for librarians by librarians provides authoritative, practical information and guidance on a wide spectrum of library processes and operations.

Books in the series are focused, describing practical and innovative solutions to a problem facing today's librarian and delivering step-by-step guidance for planning, creating, implementing, managing, and evaluating a wide range of services and programs.

The books are aimed at beginning and intermediate librarians needing basic instruction/guidance in a specific subject and at experienced librarians who need to gain knowledge in a new area or guidance in implementing a new program/service.

About the Series Editor

The **Practical Guides for Librarians** series was conceived by and is edited by M. Sandra Wood, MLS, MBA, AHIP, FMLA, Librarian Emerita, Penn State University Libraries.

M. Sandra Wood was a librarian at the George T. Harrell Library, The Milton S. Hershey Medical Center, College of Medicine, Pennsylvania State University, Hershey, PA, for over 35 years, specializing in reference, educational, and database services. Ms. Wood worked for several years as a Development Editor for Neal-Schuman Publishers.

Ms. Wood received a MLS from Indiana University and a MBA from the University of Maryland. She is a Fellow of the Medical Library Association and served as a member of MLA's Board of Directors from 1991 to 1995. Ms. Wood is founding and current editor of *Medical Reference Services Quarterly*, now in its 35th volume. She also was founding editor of the *Journal of Consumer Health on the Internet* and the *Journal of Electronic Resources in Medical Libraries* and served as editor/co-editor of both journals through 2011.

Titles in the Series

1. *How to Teach: A Practical Guide for Librarians* by Beverley E. Crane.

2. *Implementing an Inclusive Staffing Model for Today's Reference Services* by Julia K. Nims, Paula Storm, and Robert Stevens.

How to Teach

A Practical Guide for Librarians

Beverley E. Crane

PRACTICAL GUIDES FOR LIBRARIANS, No. 1

ROWMAN & LITTLEFIELD
Lanham • Boulder • New York • Toronto • Plymouth, UK
2014

Published by Rowman & Littlefield
4501 Forbes Boulevard, Suite 200, Lanham, Maryland 20706
www.rowman.com

10 Thornbury Road, Plymouth PL6 7PP, United Kingdom

British Library Cataloguing in Publication Information Available

Library of Congress Cataloging-in-Publication Data
Crane, Beverley E.
  How to teach : a practical guide for librarians / Beverley E. Crane.
    pages cm. — (Practical guides for librarians : no. 1)
  Includes bibliographical references and index.
   ISBN 978-0-8108-9105-0 (pbk. : alk. paper) — ISBN 978-0-8108-9106-7 (ebook)
1. Information literacy–Study and teaching–Handbooks, manuals, etc. 2. Information literacy–Web-based instruction–Handbooks, manuals, etc. 3. Library orientation–Handbooks, manuals, etc. 4. Library orientation–Web-based instruction–Handbooks, manuals, etc. 5. Web-based instruction–Design–Handbooks, manuals, etc. 6. Teaching–Handbooks, manuals, etc. 7. Lesson planning–Handbooks, manuals, etc. 8. Libraries and education. I. Title.
  ZA3075.C73 2014
  028.7071–dc23   2013027806

♾™ The paper used in this publication meets the minimum requirements of American National Standard for Information Sciences—Permanence of Paper for Printed Library Materials, ANSI/NISO Z39.48-1992.

Printed in the United States of America

For dedicated librarians in school, public, academic, and special libraries,
whose efforts promote lifelong learning

For my granddaughter, Natalie Johnston, a 2013 high school honors graduate
just starting on her lifelong learning journey at Georgetown University

Contents

List of Figures ix

List of Tables xi

List of Handouts xiii

Preface xv

Acknowledgments xix

CHAPTER 1 **Teaching to Learn** 1

CHAPTER 2 **Planning Instruction** 13

CHAPTER 3 **Implementing Instruction** 31

CHAPTER 4 **Types of Instruction** 49

CHAPTER 5 **Face-to-Face Presentations** 67

CHAPTER 6 **Online Instruction** 95

CHAPTER 7 **Synchronous Instruction** 115

CHAPTER 8 **Asynchronous Instruction** 137

CHAPTER 9 **What's Ahead for the Instruction Librarian?** 171

Index 175

About the Author 177

List of Figures

Figure 1.1. Job posting for librarians

Figure 1.2. Characteristics of learning

Figure 1.3. Kolb's experiential cycle of learning

Figure 1.4. Model of the information search process

Figure 2.1. ARCS model: attention, relevance, confidence, satisfaction

Figure 2.2. ADDIE model: analysis, design, development, implementation, evaluation

Figure 2.3. Bloom's taxonomy

Figure 2.4. Gagne's nine events of instruction

Figure 2.5. Information sources

Figure 3.1. Learners' individual differences

Figure 3.2. Writing objectives

Figure 3.3. Graphic organizer template

Figure 4.1. Principles to consider when creating instruction

Figure 5.1. Blogspot blog sample

Figure 7.1. *Grapes of Wrath* photo

Figure 7.2. Blackboard home page

Figure 7.3. WebEx home page

Figure 7.4. Search worksheet

Figure 8.1. YouTube Education home page

Figure 8.2. Fred Hutchinson Cancer Research Center

Figure 8.3. "Quickstart Help & Standards" guide

Figure 8.4. Pinterest 101

Figure 8.5. Pinterest example: Oakland Public Library's Teen Zone

Figure 8.6. Syracuse University Libraries virtual tour

Figure 8.7. ProQuest Dialog screenshot

Figure 8.8. LibGuides help and documentation

Figure 8.9. LibGuide visual maps

List of Tables

Table 1.1. Gardner's Multiple Intelligences

Table 1.2. URLs for Chapter 1

Table 2.1. URLs for Needs Assessment

Table 2.2. URLs for Chapter 2

Table 2.3. Library Websites

Table 2.4. Instructional Outline

Table 3.1. Instructional Techniques

Table 3.2. URLs for Chapter 3

Table 4.1. URLs for Chapter 4

Table 5.1. Resources for Web Evaluation

Table 5.2. URLs for Chapter 5

Table 6.1. URLs for Chapter 6

Table 7.1. Learning Management Systems

Table 7.2. Feature Comparison of Blackboard and WebEx

Table 7.3. Rubric for Evaluating Online Courses

Table 7.4. URLs for Chapter 7

Table 8.1. Tutorials/Screencasts

Table 8.2. Comparison of Types of Programs Used in Video Production

Table 8.3. URLs for Video Lesson

Table 8.4. URLs for Integrated LibGuide Lesson

List of Handouts

Handout 2.1. Session Evaluation

Handout 2.2. Information Sources Exercise

Handout 2.3. Self-Evaluation Checklist

Handout 3.1. Sample Training and Learning Evaluation Form

Handout 3.2. Lesson Plan Template

Handout 5.1. Criteria for Evaluating Websites

Handout 5.2. Detecting Bias

Handout 5.3. Criteria for Children to Evaluate Websites

Handout 5.4. Criteria for Evaluating Social Media Sites

Handout 5.5. Self-Evaluation Checklist

Handout 5.6. Participant Workshop Evaluation Example

Handout 5.7. Workshop Instructor Assessment

Handout 5.8. Group Participation Rubric

Handout 8.1. Sample Storyboard Template

Handout 8.2. Video Evaluation

Handout 8.3. Video Self-Evaluation Review Form

Handout 8.4. Group Critique Form

Handout 8.5. Staff Development Evaluation Form

Preface

Adults and youth today are becoming ever more keenly aware that libraries are prime sources for free access to books, magazines, e-books, DVDs, the Internet, technology, and professional assistance. Public libraries are serving as a lifeline for people trying to adapt to challenging economic circumstances, by providing technology training and online resources for employment, access to government resources, continuing education, retooling for new careers, and starting small businesses. Higher education is offering more online courses, and libraries should be at the forefront of this directional change. Special libraries are continually meeting the diverse information needs of business leaders, scientists, and colleagues.

A majority of students entering college acknowledge that they lack the research skills needed to complete assignments and be successful in an information-intensive economy. Accreditation commissions and postsecondary institutions emphasize the importance of developing students' information literacy capabilities. Librarians are being called on to meet this challenge. Yet, many are frustrated because they have not been equipped to handle the teaching needs that now face them. *How to Teach: A Practical Guide for Librarians* is designed to meet that need.

I started this book by interviewing working and retired public, academic, and special librarians to get their opinions on challenges they face and to learn from their experiences. The results were not only interesting but reinforced anecdotal evidence about teaching that I had already heard from other librarians. Although instruction librarians have most often never been trained to teach patrons or students, they have all the qualities—reference skills background, information organization, knowledge of resources, search expertise, and working with the public. The expertise lacking is the knowledge of pedagogy—how to teach. This book provides the theory, practice, advice, and materials that instruction librarians need to have the expertise and confidence to get started in this new teaching role.

With a background in education and instructional technology, I had a goal to become a trainer and create my own materials. So, I was ecstatic when I was hired by Dialog Information Services in 1989 to teach students how to search Dialog online databases—students who were, for the most part, special, academic, public, and school librarians. It was easy for me to create workshops that focused on specific objectives, provided online activities and exercises, and assessed students' learning. However, what I have learned during my twenty-four years with Dialog, whose customers come mainly from the library world, is that many librarians are now required to teach (1) patrons in public libraries who are seeking new jobs, (2) biomedical researchers who are exploring scientific sources in corporations, or (3) students who are working on their dissertations in academic libraries—and they have not been trained as I was in how to accomplish these tasks. Thus, one of my goals in writing this book is to pass some of my experiences and knowledge on to my colleagues.

⊚ Organization

How to Teach: A Practical Guide for Librarians is divided into nine chapters. Chapter 1 provides background in learning theory and strategies that are important to consider when teaching adults. Chapter 2 introduces types of instruction and how to plan your teaching to accommodate your audience. The sample plan describes a lesson to begin teaching information literacy to younger children in a public library. Instructional design is important when creating lessons, so methods to deliver instruction for different audiences and purposes form chapter 3, and the template provides a model for lesson plans in subsequent chapters. The theory and examples of library instruction in these chapters are necessary to digest before actually creating your own training. The goal for these chapters is introduce instruction librarians to the pedagogy for teaching so that they have the underpinnings to select topics and plan lessons for specific audiences with a purpose in mind.

Chapter 4 introduces the practical applications of the book with examples from public, academic, and special libraries. Two types of instruction are discussed in detail: face-to-face teaching and online instruction. Chapter 5 highlights face-to-face encounters, including workshops, small group instruction, and one-on-one teaching. Lesson plans cover evaluating websites and social media. Chapter 6 illustrates instructional strategies to employ when teaching online, whether it is a webinar, a blended class, or self-paced instruction. A lesson plan provides a model for creating online instruction. Chapter 7 emphasizes key ideas to consider when planning and teaching online. It also provides a detailed lesson plan on a major aspect of information literacy—creating search strategies. Chapter 8 focuses on self-paced online tutorials and materials, as well as how to create video, LibGuides, and more. The final lesson plan in chapter 8 integrates the different types of instruction described in earlier chapters. Chapter 9 looks ahead to what instruction librarians and their libraries face in the twenty-first century.

Each lesson plan encompasses step-by-step instructions that you can follow, as well as suggested topics that studies have shown to be most necessary to library patrons. Handouts included in the book offer ways to create objectives, present activities, and evaluate instruction. Instruction librarians can use the plans as presented or modify them to meet the individual needs of patrons at public, academic, and special libraries, as well as for different age levels. Examples in each chapter illustrate libraries using technology tools and teaching strategies. Exercises at the end of each chapter offer opportunities to practice what you have just learned, become familiar with teaching techniques, and reflect on ideas and content. Each chapter also includes an additional list of websites on the topic under discussion.

Librarians have always been in the business of lifelong learning. They are in a core position to encourage continuous learning and improvement for adults beyond whatever formal schooling they may have had. Working with patrons who are affected by the economic turmoil offers excellent opportunities, not only to build skills, but to shift the mindset to a twenty-first-century kind of thinking. Instruction librarians are expected to teach patrons, whether it is how to use library materials, find information online, use technology, or become information literate.

How to Teach is meant to fill the void in teaching knowledge that remains as librarians begin their first library positions. It is also designed to show longtime librarians how to create instruction that they are now being required to handle. The explanatory material, step-by-step explanations, examples, and model lessons should encourage librarians to try teaching their patrons, using different venues and methods. Librarians should also feel more comfortable in the teaching environment, which will translate into better learning for their patrons. The library is a place for lifelong learning for both librarians and patrons. As libraries branch out in this direction to meet the twenty-first-century needs of their patrons, librarians can lead the crusade.

Acknowledgments

Having worked for Dialog for the last twenty-four years alongside school, public, academic, and special librarians, I have become quite familiar with the changes in libraries over almost a quarter of a century. Stories abound from my librarian colleagues at Dialog, from my training classes at public and academic libraries, and from my contacts with school librarians. Creating diverse training materials from print to video as technology has changed over the years has kept me up-to-date with the challenges facing librarians. This book is the product of those stories and anecdotes and working closely with this dedicated group of educators.

I must thank all those librarians who sat down with me to answer my questions and complete questionnaires so that I could verify my beliefs about changes in the library world and the important role that teaching is now playing for today's librarians and information professionals. These dedicated professionals provided valuable insight into what they needed to meet the challenges they are currently facing in their libraries. I welcome the chance to fill some of the gaps in their education so that they can better meet these new responsibilities.

Finally, I thank Sandy Wood, also a librarian and my editor at Rowman & Littlefield who has, as always, provided valuable suggestions on the content and organization of this book. She keeps me writing! Thanks also to my librarian friends and colleagues—Ron Rodrigues, Joan Lamarque, Cathy Rimer-Surles, and Betty Jo Hibberd, among others, who shared their expertise about different aspects of librarianship with me. This book is better because of their willingness to contribute.

CHAPTER 1

Teaching to Learn

The illiterate of the 21st century will not be those who cannot read
and write, but those who cannot learn, unlearn, and relearn.

—ALVIN TOFFLER

OBJECTIVES

After completing this chapter, you will be able to

▷ Define "learning" and its characteristics

▷ Compare and contrast different theories of learning

▷ Define steps to library learning theory

▷ Identify characteristics of adult and child learners

HOW MANY online courses or workshops have you taught? What training materials have you created? As shown in figure 1.1, the 2012 library job postings for librarians require qualifications to teach courses and provide materials for library patrons.

Introduction

If you are like many librarians who are now teaching as part of their library jobs, you may never have had courses in school on how to teach—or even when you began your first library position. Even those librarians who have had the opportunity to take a course in

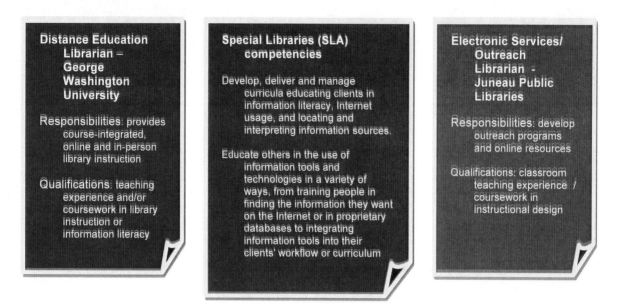

Distance Education Librarian – George Washington University

Responsibilities: provides course-integrated, online and in-person library instruction

Qualifications: teaching experience and/or coursework in library instruction or information literacy

Special Libraries (SLA) competencies

Develop, deliver and manage curricula educating clients in information literacy, Internet usage, and locating and interpreting information sources.

Educate others in the use of information tools and technologies in a variety of ways, from training people in finding the information they want on the Internet or in proprietary databases to integrating information tools into their clients' workflow or curriculum

Electronic Services/ Outreach Librarian - Juneau Public Libraries

Responsibilities: develop outreach programs and online resources

Qualifications: classroom teaching experience / coursework in instructional design

Figure 1.1. Job posting for librarians.

instruction realize that one course is inadequate preparation for teaching. In the library literature, Scott Walter (2005, 363) discusses the attention drawn to the lack of academic coursework on instruction and teaching in American Library Association–accredited library science programs and notes that "surveys conducted in the late 1990s found that barely more than one-half . . . offered even an elective course on instruction."

So, you were probably surprised when you found that your work responsibilities included technology training, teaching online courses or formal classes on library computers, or providing informal one-to-one assistance while leaning over a patron's library monitor. You are not alone.

Responses from several librarians emphasized this fact:

"Everything I learned was through on-the-job training and internal training."

"I never had a course in learning theory or how to teach while I was in library school."

"My library had five computers and patrons who needed to learn about computers. I was elected to conduct training on computer basics for a small group."

"I had a technology undergraduate degree and decided to get an MLS [master of library science]. I was a logical choice to teach about computers. I was glad, and so were my colleagues at the library who had no training."

What constitutes "training"? You might teach classes in a computer lab or online, or you might create self-paced tutorials or videos. Training encompasses all these activities. Whether you work in an academic, public, or special library, you might train library staff members, students, and the public—adults and children. You could be a volunteer. You may have a master of library science; you might not. The common factor is simply that during your library career, you probably did not plan to deal primarily with technology, teach workshops, or create learning materials.

A teaching librarian directs the growth of learners by helping them become competent or proficient in a skill or task. These instructors use coaching, instructing, and facilitating techniques to accomplish learning objectives. A skillful trainer makes it easier for learners to learn, by attempting to discover what a participant is interested in knowing, then by determining the best way to make that information available by providing the appropriate knowledge, activities, or materials. This is done by listening, asking questions, providing ideas, suggesting alternatives, and identifying possible resources. Many librarians seem to be natural trainers, as training has a lot to do with customer service and fulfilling the information needs of patrons. A background in reference skills, information organization, creating children's reading programs or teen writing sessions, knowledge of resources, online searching and evaluation, information seeking, or project planning can be useful.

To formulate strategies for teaching adults and children, you must know how individuals learn. In this chapter, you will review theories of learning—those that are new and those that have stood the test of time. You will look at a number of theories about learning, developed by psychologists, scientists, and researchers that have influenced teaching over the years. Early studies conducted primarily to see how children learned have formed the basis of research on adult learning, and you will examine these first. Next, you will review adult learning principles to understand what motivates adult learners so that you can prepare appropriate instruction. Finally, you will examine teaching strategies based on learning styles to identify ways to individualize instruction so that all learners whom you, as a librarian, teach have the best chances to succeed. The theory in this chapter provides a framework for instruction and practice that follow in the other chapters of this book.

What Is Learning?

Researchers define learning as "acquiring new, or modifying existing, knowledge, behaviors, skills, values, or preferences and may involve synthesizing different types of information" (Schacter, Gilbert, and Wegner, 2011, 264).

Learning is a complex, natural, lifelong process. It starts when we are children, and it never stops. It is active, fundamentally personal, and interactive, meaning that it also takes place in social situations. The ways that you learn, however, change as you grow and your experiences increase (see figure 1.2).

General Learning Theories

Research on ways that children and adults learn comes from noted researchers, such as B. F. Skinner, Jean Piaget, Jerome Brunner, David Kolb, Carl Rogers, and Malcolm Knowles. These researchers are identified with three major perspectives, or schools of thought, on learning: behaviorism, cognitivism, and constructivism. Brief descriptions of each theory that identify its key components can help librarians identify an appropriate learning theory, draw practical ideas from it, and apply it to their daily work. To determine the theory, they should ask themselves these questions:

- *Which theory should I choose?*
- *What is its central premise?*
- *How does it relate to other theories?*

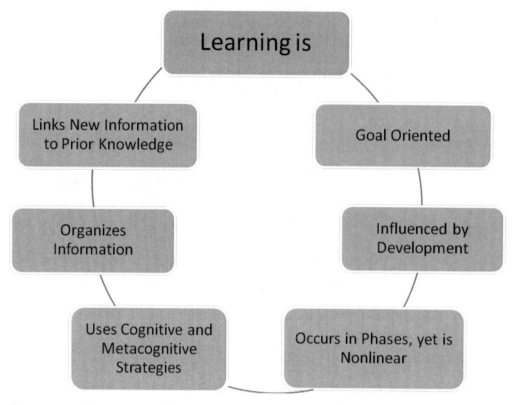

Figure 1.2. Characteristics of learning.

How Children Learn

Historically, you would first look at theory from the behaviorist school. Behaviorism was primarily developed by B. F. Skinner, and it encompasses the work of Edward Thorndike. These researchers based their theory on three assumptions: first, learning is manifested by a change in behavior; second, the environment shapes behavior; third, closeness in time of events and reinforcement are central to explaining the learning process. Behaviorists believe that learning is the acquisition of new behavior through conditioning. In *The Technology of Teaching* (1961), Skinner says that teachers have not been given an in-depth understanding of teaching and learning so that they can succeed. According to his interpretation of behaviorism, the teacher needs to clearly specify the action or performance that the student is to learn, by (1) breaking down the task into small achievable steps, going from simple to complex; (2) having the student perform each step, reinforcing correct actions; (3) adjusting instruction so that the student is always successful until the goal is finally reached; and (4) providing intermittent reinforcement to maintain the student's performance. While some classrooms still follow this approach, this theory of learning is mainly used when teaching rote types of tasks—that is, involving repetition and memorization (e.g., learning spelling words, vocabulary).

Piaget (1929), a well-known cognitive learning psychologist, pursued a theory different from that of behaviorists when he postulated that the types of knowledge that children acquired differed—namely, they became increasingly more complex as children passed through four stages of development. Piaget determined that providing activities or situations that engage learners and require them to adapt facilitates cognitive development.

Teaching methods should actively engage children and present challenges, but students should be asked to perform tasks that are just beyond their capabilities. Piaget's theories are more in tune with today's curriculum development and teaching practices.

Unlike Piaget, Jerome Brunner (1966) considered learning an active process in which individuals construct new ideas or concepts based on their current and past knowledge. In his constructivist point of view, students select and transform information, construct hypotheses, and make decisions relying on present and past experiences. Thus, curriculum should be arranged to build on current and past knowledge. Learning should focus on solving real-world problems. Collaboration and reflective thinking are important in this model. Teachers act as facilitators, presenting and encouraging multiple perspectives and helping students analyze strategies. As a result, students play a central role in controlling their own learning.

David Kolb's research (1984) focuses on the way that individuals experience learning. Kolb proposes a four-stage cycle of learning in which immediate or concrete experiences provide a basis for observations and reflections. These observations and reflections are assimilated and distilled into abstract concepts producing new implications for action, which can be actively tested and, in turn, create new experiences (see figure 1.3). Kolb indicates that experience leads individuals to reflect on what they see, hear, or touch. After reflecting, they form concepts that help them make sense of the world. They then test their concepts by experimenting.

Carl Rogers (1969) focuses on a more "humanist" approach to learning. He suggests that "needs and wants" are the most important factors to learning. He postulates that experiential learning requires personal involvement, that it should be self-initiated, and that it

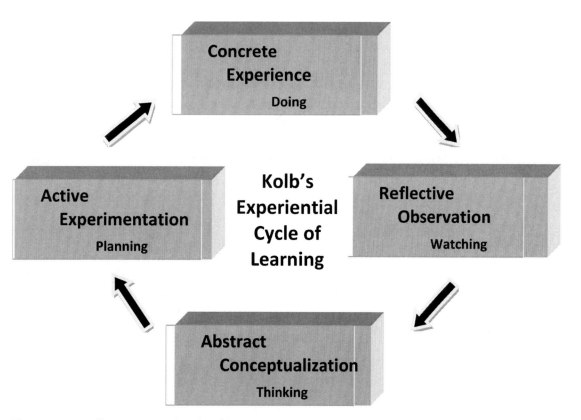

Figure 1.3. Kolb's experiential cycle of learning, 2005–2006. *Concept, David Kolb; adaptation and design, Alan Chapman.*

has far-reaching, pervasive effects on learners. The teacher's role is to facilitate learning by setting a positive, nonthreatening classroom climate and by including resources necessary for learning to take place. In other words, the teacher should not dominate the learning process. As you examine Malcolm Knowles's research next, you will see how the principles of these theorists have influenced adult learning theory.

How Adults Learn

Teaching adults is different from teaching children primarily because (1) adults are experienced learners and (2) they want usable results from learning. Malcolm Knowles (1984) published his adult learning theory and principles to explain the specific ways that adults learn. According to Knowles, adult learners are mainly self-motivated and view learning for its own sake or as a means of self-realization. Most often, adults are self-directed and expect to take responsibility for decisions. Adult learners are individuals who are in a particular stage of intellectual growth. They bring a series of experiences, values, expectations, and intentions to what learning can accomplish. Their interest in learning often has a number of competing goals and tasks, such as work and family. They already have set patterns of learning brought about by a number of years of education and employment. The primary reason for teaching adults is to help them learn, rather than teach them everything the instructor happens to know. Adult learning needs to be learner-centered.

Factors Influencing Adult Learning

As you teach or create training for adults, keep the following in mind.

Structure of learning experiences. Adults learn better when the learning is individualized and their styles are taken into account and where schedules are flexible and respond to adults' time constraints.

Learning climate. Adults prefer peer support and mutual helpfulness. The climate should be nonthreatening with a sense of trust and acceptance. Adult learners bring clear expectations to the learning environment and expect instructors to accommodate those expectations. They want to express their views and, in turn, hear the views of others.

Focus of learning. Adults need to learn experientially. They prefer active participation in the learning process. Instruction should also take into account the wide range of individuals' backgrounds; learning materials and activities should allow for different levels and types of previous experience. Finally, adults like to use reflection, analysis, and critical examination to process their experience. Thus, they value teaching methods that emphasize how-to learning and problem solving.

Need to know/goal oriented. Adults want to know why they should learn something. Adults learn best when the topic is of immediate value or relevant to their jobs or personal life.

Self-direction. Adults want to be involved in the planning and evaluation of their instruction. Since adults are self-directed, instruction should allow learners to discover things for themselves, providing guidance and helping them if they make mistakes.

Library Learning Theory

In addition to general learning theories already described, several theorists' writings relate directly to libraries and learning.

Information Search Process

Carol Kuhlthau (2004) developed the idea of the information search process in her research. She postulated that people actively and constantly construct their view of the world by assimilating and accommodating new information with what they already know or have experienced. The information search process is the user's constructive activity of finding meaning from information to extend his or her state of knowledge on a particular problem or topic. It incorporates a series of encounters with information within a space of time rather than a single reference incident (see figure 1.4).

Her learning theory contains six basic steps:

1. Initiation: Learners begin the research process by recognizing a need for information. This step is characterized by feelings of uncertainty or apprehension.
2. Selection: The learner starts by selecting a topic to research to begin the research process. Feelings of optimism or excitement may accompany this step.
3. Exploration: As the research process begins in earnest, the learner may again feel frustrated or uncertain as information seeking produces too little or too many results or if the information found does not fit with the learner's existing knowledge or beliefs.
4. Formulation: As learners gather enough information and begin to focus their information seeking, they again feel confident, and their goals become clearer.
5. Collection: This stage is where most information gathering takes place once the focus of the research is clear and well developed. At this point, learners will be efficient and effective in finding relevant resources on their subjects and integrating them into their bodies of knowledge.
6. Presentation: This is the stage at which learners prepare to present the information to others as papers, presentations, or some other uses of the findings. If the research has gone well, feelings of satisfaction, confidence, and relief are prevalent.

Model of the Information Search Process

	Initiation	Selection	Exploration	Formulation	Collection	Presentation	Assessment
Feelings (Affective)	Uncertainty	Optimism	Confusion Frustration Doubt	Clarity	Sense of direction / Confidence	Satisfaction or Disappointment	Sense of accomplishment
Thoughts (Cognitive)	vague ——————→			focused —————————————→ increased interest			Increased self-awareness
Actions (Physical)	seeking	relevant Exploring	information	seeking	pertinent Documenting	information	

Figure 1.4. Model of the information search process. *Courtesy, Carol C. Kuhlthau, from* Seeking Meaning: A Process Approach to Library and Information Services, *p. 82.*

Merrill's "First Principles of Instruction" (2010) is a well-regarded example of principles that are required for effective instruction. Learning is promoted when

1. learners are engaged in solving real-world problems,
2. existing knowledge is activated as a foundation for new knowledge,
3. new knowledge is demonstrated to the learner,
4. new knowledge is applied by the learner, and
5. new knowledge is integrated into the learner's work.

Key Points about Learning

The appropriate instructional approach should be based on the level of thinking required. Tasks requiring memorization or association might be best accomplished with behaviorist techniques. Classifying and solving problems are concepts that need cognitive strategies. The question to consider is, which theory is most effective to enable individual learners to master specific tasks? These are principles to consider in any workshops, webinars, or other types of training that you create or conduct with whoever is your audience.

Learning Style Theories

When you design training for learners, another important aspect to consider is an individual's learning style. Learning styles can be defined as characteristic methods of responding to and processing learning events as individuals experience them. Studies on learning styles consider the concept in different ways.

The visual–auditory–kinesthetic learning styles model, or inventory, classifies learners through their perceptual modality: visual, auditory, and tactile/kinesthetic. It is a simple way to explain and understand your learning style and that of others. Visual learners learn by watching and seeing. They like demonstration and will try something after they have seen how it works and what it does. They are quietly observant and like to write things down. Auditory learners learn best by hearing. They prefer to discuss various aspects of a subject. Lectures and tapes of lessons can be helpful to this type of learner. Kinesthetic learners learn by doing. They like to handle things. They remember what they did and are less likely to remember what they saw and heard. The majority of learners are mixed, meaning that they have qualities of at least two styles. Some utilize all systems equally well. By making learners aware of their best learning tools and by helping them understand how to exploit their strengths and develop their noninstinctive styles, some researchers contend that studying and learning ought to be more productive.

Howard Gardner (1983) suggests that there are seven distinct forms of intelligence that each individual possesses in varying degrees: linguistic, musical, logical–mathematical, visual–spatial, body–kinesthetic, intrapersonal, and interpersonal. According to Gardner, individuals should be encouraged to use their preferred intelligences. However, instructional activities should appeal to, and their assessment should measure, multiple forms of intelligence (see table 1.1). Gardner has continued to develop his thinking and theory from the seven original intelligences to eight or nine today.

Kolb (1984) based his discussion of learning styles on his experiential learning. He defined three stages of a person's development and suggested that as individuals mature

Table 1.1. Gardner's Multiple Intelligences

INTELLIGENCE TYPE	CAPABILITY AND PERCEPTION	DESCRIPTION
Linguistic	Words and language	Likes to read, write, listen to stories; uses language fluently
Logical–mathematical	Logic and numbers	Focuses on problem solving and reasoning; recognizes patterns and categorizes, analyzes, and interprets data
Musical	Music, sound, rhythm	Aware of rhythm and melody
Bodily–kinesthetic	Body movement control	Uses one's body to convey emotions; good at physical activities
Visual–spatial	Images and space	Stimulated through pictures, images, and colors; likes to draw; good with maps and charts
Interpersonal	Other people's feelings	Communicates well with people; likes to socialize and is often a leader
Intrapersonal	Self-awareness	Stimulated by self-reflection; likes individual, self-paced projects

through three development stages, their ability to integrate four learning styles improves. The development stages that Kolb identified are as follows:

Acquisition—birth to adolescence, development of basic abilities and cognitive structures

Specialization—schooling, early work, and personal experiences of adulthood; development of a specialized learning style shaped by social, educational, and organizational socialization

Integration—midcareer through later life, expression of nondominant learning style in work and personal life

The four-process learning cycle—concrete experience, reflective observation, abstract conceptualization, and active experimentation—flows from experience to experimentation, resulting in four learning styles:

Diverger—uses concrete experience and what it means for one's life, talks about the experience

Assimilator—reflective observation and conceptualizing, makes sense of information (the analyzer)

Converger—abstract conceptualization and active experimentation, takes the reflections and applies concepts to something practical

Accommodator—experimenter uses concrete experience, takes the practical application and forms a new experience (the doer)

Whatever influences the choice of style, the learning style preference is actually the product of two choices that individuals make. Review a diagram of Kolb's learning styles at http://www.businessballs.com/freepdfmaterials/kolb_learning_styles_diagram_colour.pdf.

And then there are opposing points of view. Toward the end of 2009, objectors to learning style theory asserted that with little large-scale scientific research into young people's education, learning styles theories and models remain largely unproven methodologies. Therefore, heavy reliance on these theories in formulating young people's education strategies is of questionable benefit and may in some cases be counterproductive. Despite objections to learning style theory, consider the ideas as you begin providing instructional resources for people young and old—for their careers, work, life, business, and management—and for teachers, trainers, managers, and leaders, helping them improve and develop their learning.

Key Points

In the first part of this chapter, you spent time reviewing learning theories relating to children and adults. To prepare environments and experiences that meet the needs of all learners, it is important to synthesize the research conducted on learning theory and learning styles to provide guidelines upon which to build training sessions. Knowing these learning theories can have a positive influence on your ability to create and deliver instruction. This brief overview is designed to help you gain a basic understanding of the principles and learning theories that can help you improve your library instruction (for additional information, see table 1.2).

Table 1.2. URLs for Chapter 1

DESCRIPTION	URL
Gardner's multiple intelligences	http://citt.ufl.edu/tools/howard-garnders-theory-of-multiple-intelligences/
Videos on multiple intelligences	http://www.youtube.com/watch?v=I2QtSbP4FRg http://www.youtube.com/channel/HCTQi4FD89c2s
Different learning styles, including Kolb	http://www.youtube.com/watch?v=9-ZiYO0dHFE
More on learning theories	http://edudemic.com/2012/12/a-simple-guide-to-4-complex-learning-theories/
Visual on learning theories	http://edudemic.com/wp-content/uploads/2012/12/theories-of-learning-fixed.jpg
Adult learning theory	http://www.qotfc.edu.au/resource/?page=65375

EXERCISES: Now You Try It . . .

The questions that follow let you see how well you have comprehended and can apply the ideas about learning theories and learning styles discussed in this chapter.

1. Set up a learning log in which you can map out the information discussed in each chapter, for use when you are tasked to create your own training sessions and materials. Discuss the following:
   a. Which learning theory do you adhere to most (e.g., behaviorist, cognitive)?
   b. Identify characteristics of that theory that you feel most comfortable with and why.

    c. Give an example of a situation in which you felt that you could have learned better if another approach had been used. Explain and indicate why.
2. As you review learning style theories, which approach to learning styles did you select as most like yours and why?
    a. Which is your preferred general learning style (or styles)?
    b. Narrowing to Gardner's learning styles, which is your preferred style (or styles)?
    c. What types of activities enable you to learn best?
    d. Have you taken learning styles into consideration when working with children or adults? Provide an example.

References

Brunner, Jerome. 1966. *Toward a Theory of Instruction.* Cambridge, MA: Harvard University Press.

Gardner, Howard. 1983. *Frames of Mind: Theory of Multiple Intelligences.* New York: Basic Books

Knowles, Malcolm. 1984. *The Adult Learner: A Neglected Species.* 3rd ed. Houston, TX: Gulf.

Kolb, D. A. 1984. *Experiential Learning.* Englewood Cliffs, NJ: Prentice Hall.

Kuhlthau, C. C. 2004. *Seeking Meaning: A Process Approach to Library and Information Services.* 2nd ed. Westport, CT: Libraries Unlimited.

Merrill, M. D. 2010. "First Principles of Instruction." In *Instructional Design Theories and Models III*, edited by C. M. Reigeluth and A. Carr, 47–49. Mahwah, NJ: Erlbaum.

Piaget, Jean. 1929. *The Child's Conception of the World.* New York: Harcourt Brace Jovanovich.

Rogers, Carl R. 1969. *Freedom to Learn: A View of What Education Might Become.* Columbus, OH: Merrill.

Schacter, Daniel L., Daniel T. Gilbert, and Daniel M. Wegner. 2011. *Psychology, 2nd edition.* New York: Worth.

Skinner, B. F. 1961. *The Technology of Teaching.* New York: Wiley.

Walter, S. 2005. "Improving Instruction: What Librarians Can Learn from the Study of College Teaching." In *Currents and Convergence: Navigating the Rivers of Change—Proceedings of the Twelfth National Conference of the Association of College and Research Libraries, April 7–10, 2005, Minneapolis, Minnesota*, edited by H. A. Thompson, 363–79. Chicago: Association of College and Research Libraries. http://ala.org/acrl/files/conferences/pdf/waltr05.pdf.

Further Reading

Keller, J. M. 1987. "Development and Use of the ARCS Model of Motivational Design." *Journal of Instructional Development* 10 (10): 2–10.

Kuhlthau, C. C. 1991. "Inside the Search Process: Information Seeking from the User's Perspective." *Journal of the American Society for Information Science* 42 (5): 361–71.

Kuhlthau, C., L. Maniotes, and A. Caspari. 2007. *Guided Inquiry: Learning in the 21st Century.* Westport, CT: Libraries Unlimited.

CHAPTER 2

Planning Instruction

OBJECTIVES

After completing this chapter, you will be able to

▷ Identify instructional design models

▷ Describe steps in the instructional design process

▷ Design teaching strategies based on adult learning needs

WITH THE growth of instructional initiatives and influence across libraries of all kinds, expectations for librarians to develop teaching expertise have heightened. Librarians who teach now find themselves faced with the demand to connect with students, to make libraries and information literacy knowledge meaningful, and to create learning opportunities that are memorable and long lasting.

Today's Libraries

More Americans than ever are turning to their libraries for access to essential technology services not found elsewhere in the community, including free computer and Internet access, technology training, and assistance with job seeking and e-government services. A recent Pew Internet & American Life Project report (2013) found that the majority of Americans aged sixteen and older (58 percent) have a library card and even more (69 percent) say that the library is important to them and their families.

Other key findings indicate the following:

- 62 percent of public libraries are the only source of free public access to computers and the Internet in their communities, with an increase to 70 percent in rural communities;

- 60 percent of libraries have increased use of public Internet computers;
- 76 percent of libraries offer access to e-books, an increase of 9 percent from last year;
- 91 percent of public libraries provide free Wi-Fi, and 74 percent report that use of Wi-Fi increased in 2011; and
- 65 percent of libraries have an insufficient number of public computers to meet demand, an increase to 87 percent in urban libraries.

As a result of the increased usage of the library, more patrons now need instruction on how to find or use resources contained in it. For example, the Environmental Protection Agency National Library Network is expanding its topic offerings and exploring alternatives to its current webinar technology to allow playback of its training sessions. In addition, it plans to improve the curriculum to provide more targeted sessions customized to the needs of individuals and small groups. The agency is also looking at on-demand modules and contextual help within online services so that patrons know how to access this information.

Today's Librarians

Today's librarians are involved in a variety of challenging activities. Academic librarians, for example, meet the information needs of students, faculty, researchers, and other library users. Typically, they collaborate with classroom faculty, computer specialists, and instructional developers; they create campuswide information literacy programs; and they develop and teach library instruction sessions or courses in the classroom and increasingly online.

Librarians in public libraries—especially in the current, changing job market, where employees may hold ten to fifteen positions during their careers—help prepare their patrons for the reality of continuous learning and teach them how to learn. Patrons may call on librarians to provide training on technology, workshops to help them upgrade their work skills, or online courses on how to find information on health concerns or tax matters.

Traditionally, special librarians—whether in businesses, law firms, or government organizations—have helped employees with their research, prior art, patents on new drugs, and competitors, to name a few. Today, researchers, attorneys, and legal assistants are expected to conduct more of their own research, and they need training on how to plan a search, identify databases, and find specific content sources. The librarian who offers orientation and training to new employees, who anticipates the research and learning needs of longtime employees, and who is able to interpret and train patrons on new technology is a librarian who offers a company or organization valuable skills.

A typical master of library and information science encompasses core courses in information retrieval, information organizations and management, research methods in library and information science, advanced topics, and the thesis. Depending on the type of library of interest, students can then select from electives such as reference and information services, government information sources, information technology tools and applications, cataloging and organization of information, and issues related to academic, public, or special libraries. However, if offered at all, an elective may be the only option in the design and implementation of instructional strategies (i.e., planning, teaching, and assessment of learning activities). This part of the curriculum has been sadly neglected over the years, yet graduates are often expected to have these skills in their first job. The ability to train therefore often falls short of expected results despite the librarian's best intentions. Knowing how to create workshops, one-on-one training, online courses, and self-paced instruction makes the chances for success that much better.

In this chapter, you will consider important issues that relate to preparing instruction and strategies to design training especially for adult learners. You will also review steps necessary to create effective instruction. Understanding "training that works" and considering the learning theory presented in chapter 1 will make it easier for you to teach patrons, students, and colleagues in your libraries.

⊚ What Is Instructional Design?

In psychology and education, learning theories help individuals understand the process of learning. Instructional design is a way of planning instruction considering the learner, the end goal or product, and the evaluation and assessments. It is the entire process of analyzing learning needs and goals and designing a delivery system to meet those needs. It includes developing instructional materials, creating activities, and trying out and evaluating all instruction and learner activities. It includes the systematic application of strategies and techniques derived from behavioral, cognitive, and constructivist theories to the solution of instructional problems.

Instructional Design Models

Having dealt with all kinds of patrons entering your library, you know that one size does not fit all! You may be instructing children or teens, senior citizens or nonnative speakers, as well as various levels of search expertise or knowledge of the library. You may receive questions on how to set up a Facebook account, search for symptoms of diabetes, or find 2013 tax information. How to create instruction to accommodate these differences can be overwhelming. However, do not despair. Looking at some basic models in instructional design will help you get started.

ARCS Model

A model that can be easily adopted for library user education is Keller's (1987) ARCS model, a problem-solving approach to design learning environments to stimulate and sustain individuals' motivation to learn.

The ARCS model of motivation considers how to gain and keep attention during the learning process. It has been used and validated by teachers and trainers in elementary and secondary schools, colleges, and universities, as well as in adult learning settings in corporations, government agencies, nonprofit organizations, and the military—in other words, in most settings in which there is a requirement for people to learn. It has also been used around the world, especially in Asia, Europe, and Latin America. Numerous research reports verify its validity and usefulness.

This simple model consists of four steps for promoting and sustaining motivation in the learning process. It provides a good summary of the issues to be considered when designing learning material. Motivation occurs during learning while using these elements of ARCS:

Attention: if you gain and keep their attention

Relevance: when content is relevant to their interests and needs

Confidence: when the content is structured so that they feel they can be successful

Satisfaction: when they feel that they have gained some sort of satisfaction from the learning experience, in either enjoyment or achievement

Working to keep students motivated is crucial to their learning, so it is important to design the content and learning environment to best achieve that goal (see figure 2.1).

The ADDIE Model

Steven Bell (Bell and Shank 2007, 2), who introduced the concept of "blended librarianship," defines instructional design as "the systematic creation of an educational experience that will help students achieve a specified set of learning outcomes." The ADDIE model was developed by the Department of Defense in 1975 (Clark 2010) and consists of the components listed in figure 2.2.

Attention	Relevance	Confidence	Satisfaction
Perceptual Arousal Provide novelty and surprise	**Goal Orientation** Present objectives and useful purpose of instruction and specific methods for successful achievement	**Learning Requirements** Inform students about learning and performance requirements and assessment criteria	**Intrinsic Reinforcement** Encourage and support intrinsic enjoyment of the learning experience
Inquiry Arousal Stimulate curiosity by posing questions or problems to solve	**Motive Matching** Match objectives to student needs and motives	**Successful Opportunities** Provide challenging and meaningful opportunities for successful learning	**Extrinsic Rewards** Provide positive reinforcement and motivational feedback
Variability Incorporate a range of methods and media to meet students' varying needs	**Familiarity** Present content in ways that are understandable and that related to the learners' experiences and values	**Personal Responsibility** Link learning success to students' personal effort and ability	**Equity** Maintain consistent standards and consequences for success

Figure 2.1. ARCS model: attention, relevance, confidence, satisfaction. *From "Instructional Design" entry in Wikipedia, created by Kas307.*

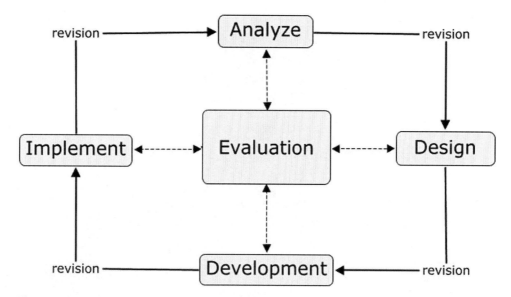

Figure 2.2. ADDIE model: analysis, design, development, implementation, evaluation.

Analysis: process that clarifies what is to be learned by what audience

Design: stage that involves planning how the material is to be delivered to the learner

Development: creation of learning materials, formative and summative evaluation

Implementation: delivery of learning materials to the learner

Evaluation: stage at which the entire process is evaluated, including assessing learner outcomes

Bloom's Taxonomy

Benjamin Bloom (1956), an educator whose research has affected how educators think about the way people learn, defined types of learning on a hierarchy of skills (see figure 2.3). His *Taxonomy of Educational Objectives for the Cognitive Domain* is designed to increase retention and promote in-depth thinking. His hierarchy starts with memorizing facts or understanding meaning at the low end and evaluating and creating that requires the learner to go beyond what is written. Information skills are tools for inquiry; individuals must find information, discern what is important in a body of facts, and restructure information relevant to a given situation. Today's citizens must be active critical thinkers to compare evidence, evaluate competing claims, and make sensible decisions. Bloom outlines the following cognitive activities, organized from least to greatest complexity:

Remember—describe, find, name, list

Understand—explain, discuss, predict, restate

Apply—illustrate, examine, classify, solve

Analyze—compare, contrast, investigate

Evaluate—justify, recommend, decide, assess

Create—invent, design, imagine, construct

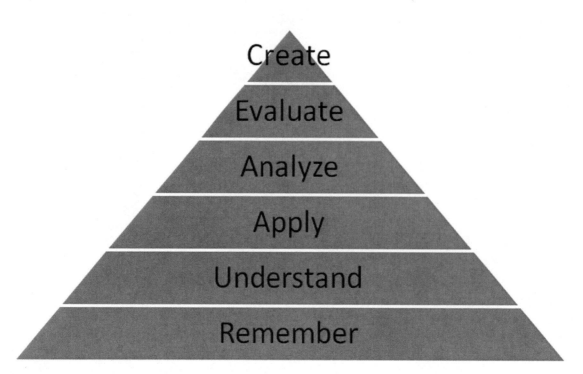

Figure 2.3. Bloom's taxonomy.

Gagne's Nine Events of Instruction

Robert Gagne's (1985) nine events of instruction correlate with how the cognitive processes in the brain affect learning. Gagne conceived the following nine events to illustrate how instructors can best facilitate learning (see figure 2.4):

1. Gain the attention of the learner—to prepare for learning and to motivate the learner
2. Inform the learner of the objective—to be explicit about what is to be learned
3. Stimulate the recall of prior learning—to help integrate new material into existing knowledge
4. Present new content material—what is to be learned prescribes the content delivery
5. Provide guided learning—to aid students in practicing and integrating knowledge
6. Elicit performance—to demonstrate the learner's recently acquired knowledge
7. Provide feedback—to help the learner improve performance
8. Assess outcomes—to evaluate the learner's performance
9. Enhance retention and transfer of new knowledge—to aid students in integrating knowledge

Components to Instructional Design

Many viable approaches to course design exist. Most approaches involve assessing the need; articulating objectives, goals, or outcomes; designing assignments; selecting instructional formats; and developing assessments. The ADDIE model mentioned earlier illustrates a more detailed view of the various components.

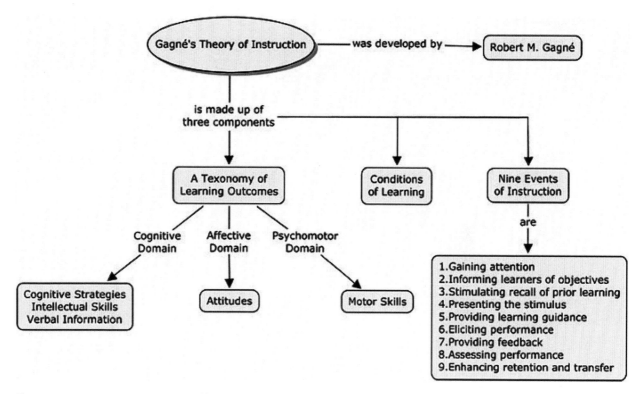

Figure 2.4. Gagne's nine events of instruction.

Step 1: Analysis

Every well-planned learning initiative should start with a thorough analysis to clearly identify the learning needs that a solution must address. A needs assessment helps libraries understand user requirements in general and the types of instruction that may address those needs. Through an audience analysis, you can determine who will participate in your training, what characteristics the potential attendees have, and what these groups of learners want to know. This will enable you to create a list of questions to assess learners' expertise on the task that you want to teach, as well as their prior knowledge, motivation, and goals. Libraries use a variety of assessment tools, such as formal and informal patron surveys, observation, research and existing data (including website statistics), and focus groups of both staff and patrons (see table 2.1).

In an information- and Internet-driven age where information, services, and resources are increasingly available only online, people who lack digital knowledge and skills struggle. A 2011–2012 survey of public libraries conducted by the American Library Association (Hoffman, Bertot, and Davis, 2012) found that 36 percent of public libraries reported increased numbers of patrons enrolling in technology training classes and requests for one-on-one assistance, with many requests from those who lacked basic computer skills. The results from a 2010 Pew Research Center survey reported that only 50 percent of rural households had broadband at home, compared to 70 percent of urban families (Smith, 2010). The results of these surveys suggest that communities across the United States depend on public libraries for physical access to technology and infrastructure, electronic content, and information professionals trained to help people find and use the information most relevant to their needs.

Table 2.1. URLs for Needs Assessment

DESCRIPTION	URL
Library services and technology—Alaska state plan	http://www.library.state.ak.us/pdf/anc/LSTAStatePlanRevision2009.pdf
Utah State Library	http://library.utah.gov/programs/training/documents/Training%20Needs%20Assessment%202012.pdf
Survey documents	http://www.webjunction.org/documents/webjunction/Sample_Information_Gathering_Tools.html

As a result of a needs analysis in a public library, for example, topics to cover may emerge:

Content—employment issues (job seeking, resume writing, and completion of online job applications), social service and government needs (access to outside resources, such as English-as-a-second-language classes, immigration appointments, youth programs, food assistance, tax help, legal information), educational needs (homework help, research needs, information on schools and colleges), business needs (directories, research, small business development)

Skill improvement—computer use, including basics such as accessing and navigating the Internet and using e-mail; intermediate skills, such as uploading and downloading files, scanning, social networking, and using other Internet-based tools; library usage skills, including knowledge of library services, materials, and programs; use of library technology, including basic skills such as searching the online catalog, printing at the library, and using the self-checkout machines; and more intermediate skills, including advanced catalog searches, use of databases, and using assistive technology

Step 2: Design

Design is based on the analysis phase, in conjunction with the theories and models of instructional design, and it ends in a model of the training process you will create. It begins with writing a learning objective, one as simple as "After this tutorial, learners will be able to successfully renew their library materials using the online form." Besides learning objectives, tasks should be identified and broken down into manageable chunks. This blueprint should contain assessment instruments, exercises, content, subject matter, a lesson plan, and media selection. You will also want to document the project's instructional, visual, and technical design strategy.

Step 3: Development

Development is the phase where a procedure is developed for training the facilitators and the learners. It elaborates and builds on the learning objectives and steps that were produced in the design phase. One of the biggest factors for deciding on the goals, objectives, and content of the instructional program will be the clients involved, because their level of education and knowledge about a topic will guide the content of the program. Included within this phase are learner activities to accomplish the objectives, the delivery system to reach the objectives, experiences to help patrons learn or know what steps to take, and what will motivate users to learn and perform. The result could be instructional—it could be a workshop, printed material, or courseware; it could contain various media and instructional content, such as software, lesson outlines, and video; and it could include activities that will aid learners in their quest for better performance.

Step 4: Implementation

Implementation is the phase where learning and training products, processes, and services are actually delivered to the learners. The instructional content must improve performance, support all training and learning needs, and ensure that the learners see the training as important and doable so that they are motivated to engage in it.

Step 5: Evaluation

Evaluation consists of two parts: formative and summative. Formative evaluations can judge the value or worth of the processes or activities. This diagnostic testing includes a range of formal and informal assessment procedures employed before and during the learning process to modify teaching and learning activities to improve learner attainment. It typically involves qualitative feedback (rather than scores) from both student and teacher that focuses on the details of content and performance. It is commonly contrasted with summative assessment, which seeks to monitor educational outcomes, often for purposes of external accountability. A summative evaluation is performed at the end of the instructional design process and focuses on the outcome.

Evaluation is important because by knowing the positive and negative aspects of the program, the instruction can be improved and delivered more successfully the next time. Evaluations are also a way to get ideas for future programs and can be used to market other programs. Depending on the type of program being evaluated, the content of the evaluation can vary. Written evaluations are most common, and you will have to decide if they should be anonymous or if the opportunity for follow-up with the patron would be helpful. They can take many forms: rubrics, checklists, multiple choice, and questionnaire. They can also be learner self-evaluations, training session evaluation, and instructor self-evaluation. Handout 2.1 provides a sample assessment questionnaire.

Lesson Plan: Applying Gagne's Events of Instruction

The following example, from one of my face-to-face workshops, could be adjusted for a group of senior citizens in a public library who are planning a Google search, a college class that is becoming acquainted with an academic library's resources, or a special library's information professional who is training employees to search its database collection.

This example focuses on a group of six to twelve upper elementary school students in an after-school session at a small public library. Their goal is to learn how to use library resources. The instruction librarian will apply Gagne's nine events of instruction.

HANDOUT 2.1. Session Evaluation

The information you supply will be used to improve the quality of instruction.

Name: _____

Date: _____

Course name: _____ Course number: _____

Instructor: _____

Circle the number that most nearly reflects your opinion for each question (1 = *not at all / low*, 4 = *very much so / high*). Use the back of the form if you have additional comments.

1. Were the objectives of this course relevant to the knowledge/skill requirements of your job?   1 2 3 4

2. Were the course materials useful and of good quality?   1 2 3 4

3. How would you rate the delivery skills of the instructor?   1 2 3 4

4. Was the course content presented in a clear and understandable manner?   1 2 3 4

5. What is your confidence level to use what you learned in this course back on the job?   1 2 3 4

Additional comments: _____

_____

_____

_____

_____

_____

_____

Step 1: Prepare for Learning and Motivating the Students

Ask questions to find out where the children look for information. For example, "If you are planning a trip this week, where will you look to make sure the weather will be good for traveling?" Or, "For your homework assignment, where did you look to complete the task?"

Brainstorm answers to the following questions on a whiteboard or a large paper to assess their prior knowledge:

- "What information have you needed in the last week?"
- "What questions have you tried to answer?"
- "Have you tried any new sources to find answers? Which ones?"
- "What was the quickest and easiest way to find the solution to your problem?"

Step 2: Be Clear about What Is to Be Learned

State objectives for the next activity in the form of what students will accomplish—in this case, they will be able to identify and find a source in the library to answer one specific question. Some possible responses might be "ask the librarian," "use the computer," or "check specific books or magazines."

Step 3: Integrate New Material into Existing Knowledge

Draw a circle on the whiteboard and ask students to list all the sources where they have obtained information in the last twenty-four hours (see figure 2.5).

Step 4: Present a Stimulus

Divide the children into groups or pairs, and ask each group to write down at least three questions—practical ones they really want to know answers to (use handout 2.2). Students will list their questions and the sources they will use to find the information.

Step 5: Provide Guidance

Provide a model. A model question and sources are listed for you in handout 2.2.

Step 6: Elicit Responses

For ten minutes, have each group brainstorm its list of questions and sources on large pieces of paper.

Step 7: Provide Feedback

Tell groups to select a spokesperson to read their questions and possible sources; have other groups provide additional sources. Each group will then select one of its questions to answer using library resources. Each has fifteen minutes to identify the source (or sources) and find answers to the question. Another option would be to assign one question for each group that requires the use of a different source (or sources).

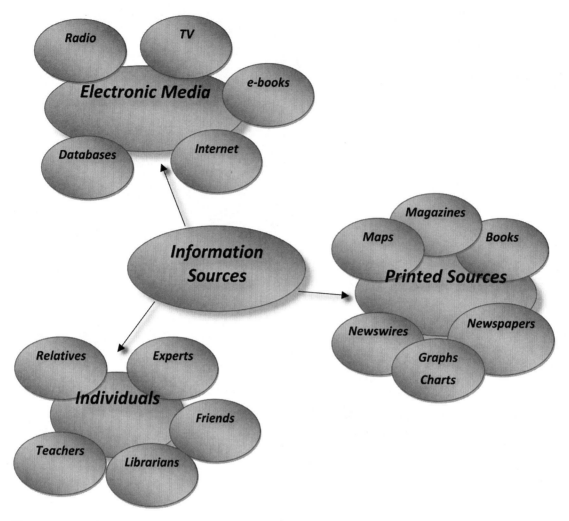

Figure 2.5. Information sources.

Step 8: Assess Performance

Monitor the participants as they look for the sources. Note the processes that they use to answer the questions, and make suggestions as they work. Groups then report their results describing the problems and successes that they had finding the sources that provided relevant answers. Following discussion, distribute handout 2.3. Children can assess their progress on the sheet. The results will also aid you in modifying and adapting future activity content and procedures.

Step 9: Enhance Retention and Transfer

At the end of the session, ask students to find information to answer a question that arises during the week and to list the sources used. The steps just outlined, suggested by Gagne, represent an organized way of learning about resources contained in the library, by answering questions important to the children. This same exercise could be used with any age group with a variety of questions.

HANDOUT 2.2. Information Sources Exercise

Directions: Answer the following questions. Provide a list of sources you used to find the answers. Suggest other sources that you did not use.

Questions	Answers	Sources
In your study of Japan's tsunami in Geography class this week, what sources did you use to find information about the tsunami that hit Japan?		
Model Question	**Model Answer**	**Model Sources**
What is a tsunami?		Internet, TV news
How did it happen?		Weather forecasts, TV, librarian
What were the results in Japan?		Newspapers, newswires
How did it affect the people?		Internet
Question	**Answer**	**Sources**

HANDOUT 2.3. Self-Evaluation Checklist

Directions: Please check the most appropriate answer for each statement.

Category	Beginning	Developing	Accomplished	Exemplary
I can distinguish among different information sources.				
I can think of at least five sources to look at to find information.				
I can use the Internet to find answers to my questions.				
I can use the databases in the library to find answers to my questions.				
I can find printed sources in the library to answer my questions.				
I feel confident about knowing where to look in the library for different types of information.				

Key Points

After reviewing instructional design based on behaviorism, cognitivism, and constructivism in chapter 1, you can see that it is best not to advocate one learning theory but stress that instructional strategy and content depend on the level of the learners. In fact, there is a place for each theory within the practice of instructional design, depending on the situation and environment. For example, the instructional approach used for novice learners may not be sufficiently stimulating for a learner who is familiar with the content. In a business environment, the designer may be required to establish and meet the objectives of that business, or in an academic setting, the librarian may be challenged to provide material that fosters an individual to find divergent approaches to problem solving. Whichever situation librarians find themselves in, they will require a thorough understanding of learning theories and instructional design models to enable them to provide the appropriate learning environment for a diverse group of patrons. Table 2.2 contains more information on the main points of this chapter.

Table 2.2. URLs for Chapter 2

DESCRIPTION	URL
ARCS model strategies	https://sites.google.com/site/elearningsnippets/a-wiki-page/arcs-model-of-motivation
Instructional system design based on the ADDIE model	http://www.nwlink.com/~donclark/hrd/sat.html
Gardner's multiple intelligences	http://citt.ufl.edu/tools/howard-garnders-theory-of-multiple-intelligences/
San Francisco Public Library needs assessment report	http://www.webjunction.org/content/dam/WebJunction/Documents/webjunction/SFPL-Patron-Needs-Assessment.pdf
Instructional design and what motivates people to learn	http://www.upsidelearning.com/blog/index.php/2011/02/10/instructional-design-for-beginners-what-motivates-people-to-learn/
Brain rules and how they affect motivation and learning	http://www.webjunction.org/content/dam/WebJunction/Documents/webJunction/New-Learning-Docs-1.pdf
Libraries Services in the Digital Age report from the Pew Research Center	http://libraries.pewinternet.org/2013/04/04/libraries-of-the-future/
A five-part report from the Pew Research Center on the role of libraries in people's and community's lives	http://libraries.pewinternet.org/2013/01/22/part-1-the-role-of-libraries-in-peoples-lives-and-communities/

Note. ARCS = attention, relevance, confidence, satisfaction; ADDIE = analysis, design, development, implementation, evaluation.

Reinforce what you learned in chapter 2 by trying the following exercises:

1. Review several library websites (e.g., American Library Association, Special Libraries Association, other public or university libraries). In your journal, list the name, URL, and at least three instructional materials that you think might be useful in your library (see table 2.3).
2. Practice developing an instructional outline based on one of the models in this chapter—ADDIE, ARCS, Gagne, or Bloom.
   a. From your library experience, select several topics on which you might have to instruct your patrons. Review these topics with your colleagues, prioritize them, and select one to develop further.
   b. Create your outline for the topic you plan to teach (see table 2.4).

Table 2.3. Library Websites

NAME OF LIBRARY	URL	DESCRIPTION OF MATERIAL	BENEFITS

Table 2.4. Instructional Outline

TOPIC	——
Analysis	Who is the audience? Does the audience want to learn about this subject? Why/why not?
Design	What are the goals and objectives? Describe content.
Development	What are the learner activities? What media will you use? What is the delivery method? What potential challenges do you anticipate? Write lesson plan.
Implementation	What motivational techniques will you use? Create exercises.
Evaluation	What type of evaluation will you employ? Write questions for formative and summative evaluation.

References

Bell, S. J., and J. D. Shank. 2007. *Academic Librarianship by Design: A Blended Librarian's Guide to the Tools and Techniques*. Chicago: American Library Association.

Bloom, Benjamin, S., ed. 1956. *Taxonomy of Educational Objectives*. New York: David McKay.

Clark, D. 2010. "ADDIE Model." http://www.nwlink.com/~donclark/history_isd/addie.html.

Gagne, R. M. 1985. *The Condition of Learning*. 4th ed. New York: Holt, Rinehart & Winston.

Hoffman, Judy, John Carlo Bertot, and Denise M. Davis. 2012. "Libraries Connect Communities: Public Library Funding and Technology Access Study 2011–2012." *American Libraries*, June, digital supplement. http://viewer.zmags.com/publication/4673a369.

Keller, J. M. 1987. "Development and Use of the ARCS Model of Motivational Design." *Journal of Instructional Development* 10:2–10.

Krathwohl, David R. 2002. "A Revision of Bloom's Taxonomy: An Overview." *Theory into Practice* 41 (4): 212–18.

Pew Internet & American Life Project. 2013. *Library Services in the Digital Age*. Washington, DC: Pew Research Center. http://libraries.pewinternet.org/2013/01/22/library-services/.

Smith, Aaron. 2010. *Home Broadband 2010*. Washington, DC: Pew Research Center. http://pewinternet.org/Reports/2012/Home-Broadband-2010.aspx.

Further Reading

Colborn, Nancy Wootten. 2011. "Introduction to Instructional Design: A Brief Primer." *Indiana Libraries* 30 (1): 15–19.

CHAPTER 3

Implementing Instruction

OBJECTIVES

When you finish this chapter, you will be able to

▷ Identify specific considerations in teaching adults

▷ Develop, implement, and demonstrate effective lesson planning

▷ Apply knowledge of learning styles and instructional strategies in the selection, design, and customization of instructional materials, resources, and media

▷ Apply Bloom's taxonomy to course design, objective development, and student evaluation

▷ Write student learning outcomes and performance objectives

▷ Construct a variety of methods for student evaluation

▷ Describe how to deliver training

▷ Discuss issues important to giving a presentation

S AN INSTRUCTION librarian with the potential to enhance student or patron learning and increase the relevance of libraries for teaching and learning, you have the opportunity to guide and lead the profession to new heights. As you pursue this path to a teacher identity, you will connect more deeply with learners and participate more fully in the learning process. As you influence the teaching practices of your library colleagues and affect the instructional role of libraries, you will influence the learning of your patrons as well as libraries and their future.

⊚ Instruction Librarian: Trainer, Instructor, Coach, or Facilitator?

More Americans than ever are turning to their libraries. The 2011–2012 *Public Library Funding and Technology Access Study* (Hoffman, Bertot, and Davis, 2012) highlights how strategic vision and careful management have helped U.S. public libraries weather the storm of the Great Recession, supporting their role as a lifeline to the technology resources and training essential to social networking and full participation in the nation's economy.

Instruction librarians are needed now more than ever before. According to the Association of College and Research Libraries (2007), an *instruction librarian* refers to any librarian with instruction responsibilities. Learning is achieved by focusing on the learners. In addition to the instruction created, learning is brought about by skillful trainers who can facilitate learning. The person who delivers instruction must have a repertoire of skills to not only help participants learn the subject but, depending on the circumstances, teach to the needs of the audience. That person might be called a *trainer*, *instructor*, *coach*, or *facilitator*. Although these terms are not synonymous, they are often used interchangeably. The delivery methods are slightly different, as the following definitions show:

> *Trainer*—directs the growth of learners by making them qualified or proficient in a skill or task
>
> *Instructor*—gives knowledge or information to learners in a systematic manner
>
> *Coach*—instructs, demonstrates, directs, guides, and prompts learners; generally concerned with methods rather than concepts
>
> *Facilitator*—guides a team toward the results that it wants to achieve so that the team maintains or improves its competency to achieve results

Characteristics of Successful Instruction

Think back to your favorite teacher—one who made an impression on you, who made you feel comfortable in the classroom, who made it easy for you to learn the content, who motivated you to learn, who kept you engaged during the class, and who was fair to all students. These are attributes that you want for yourself as you begin planning instructional sessions. Consider these important general principles:

- Offer a number of options to employ different learning styles and levels of development, including prior knowledge and experience, motivation to learn, cognitive abilities, and circumstances under which participants will be learning (see chapter 1 for more on learning styles). Because there are significant differences in the way that individuals learn, the most effective instruction offers choices that allow them to match styles with experience.
- Invite participants to collaborate, offering suggestions that meet their needs as you create your instruction and materials. Training should include input from participants regarding content and, if possible, a variety of delivery formats, giving interested persons options on how they will acquire the material.
- Involve participants in team learning during and following actual instructional sessions. Studies (e.g., Baker, 2010) indicate that the transfer of new skills is far more

likely to occur when individuals work in pairs and employ peer coaching. Working together can also reduce stress in learning something new.

- Enable participants to engage in experience-based opportunities; this means learning from doing and exploring. According to research (e.g., McKinney, 2010), active involvement leads to understanding, comfort, and commitment.
- Consider the feelings, fears, and anxieties that learners may experience with new material. The instructor must provide specific strategies for easing stress. Pacing is also essential because participants may reach a saturation point with new material at different stages.
- Provide different types of sessions to take into account age and levels of expertise to increase the chances of successful outcomes.

Best Practices for Instruction Librarians

The success of professional teachers does not "just happen." The road to success requires commitment and practice. Instruction librarians should contemplate these best practices:

- Know the basics of design and delivery—assessing needs, developing objectives, creating an agenda, selecting appropriate activities, providing for transfer, and designing and conducting evaluation activities.
- After assessing needs, select or create appropriate minilearning sessions that can be delivered as just-in-time learning.
- Understand diverse clients and their different learning styles.
- Develop activities that increasingly involve active experiential learning and debriefings.
- Provide more than one delivery system, particularly online when conducting e-learning.
- Use learner-centered instruction, especially self-directed learning, to create better ways to include opportunities for reflection, clarification, and guidance for learners.
- Use reflective practice skills to make sense of the learners' situations, tailoring learning solutions to their learning needs and developing and nurturing collaborative communities of practice.

Delivering Instruction

For anyone who teaches regularly, it is easy to recognize the aspects of teaching that are similar to acting: the preparation, the practice, the warming up of the voice, the nerves, the sweaty palms, and the vulnerability that comes with setting oneself up for approval or disapproval. Teachers, like actors, often summon charm or dynamism from within, to exude a presence and authority for their audience. There are two main methods for presenting instructional content: *deductively*, having learners work from general information to examples, and *inductively*, giving learners examples from which to create general principles. Knowing your audience and understanding its needs will help you provide the right kind of instruction in the right way. Development of trainers should include demonstrating multiple approaches to delivering the same information.

There are different types of training (see chapter 4) you should be familiar with—small group sessions, such as research consultations or appointments; one-on-one tutorials, including a reference interview; face-to-face workshops in the library or campus classrooms (see chapter 5); web-based training using blended instruction (see chapter 7); and self-paced materials, such as job aids, LibGuides, and videos (see chapter 8). As indicated, you will find more information on these instructional methods in the chapters of this book.

Instruction for Libraries

To a greater or lesser degree, depending on the type of library, the audience, and the method of instruction, there are a number of areas to consider when you start to teach. For those who have performed this role, you may know some of these techniques, but it is important to continue to refine your craft. To be effective in an academic, public, or special library, instruction librarians should increase their expertise in the following.

Subject Expertise

The following are primarily for academic and special librarians.

- Keep current with basic theories, methodologies, and topics in assigned and related subject areas, and incorporate those ideas, as relevant, when planning instruction.
- Identify core primary and secondary sources within a subject area or related disciplines, and promote the use of those resources through instruction.
- Use the vocabulary for the subject and related disciplines with students and when working with departmental faculty.
- Describe the role of information literacy in academia to patrons, programs, and departments served.
- Collaborate with classroom faculty to integrate appropriate information literacy competencies, concepts, and skills into library instruction sessions, assignments, and course content.
- Communicate with classroom faculty and administrators to collaboratively plan and implement the incremental integration of information literacy competencies and concepts within a subject discipline curriculum.
- Keep aware of student assignments and the role of the library in completing the assignments.
- Design effective assessments of student learning, and use the data collected to guide personal teaching and professional development.

Instructional Design Skills

- Collaborate by defining expectations and desired learning outcomes to determine appropriate information literacy proficiencies and resources to be introduced in library instruction.
- Sequence information in a lesson plan to guide the instruction session, course, workshop, or other instructional material.
- Create learner-centered course content, and incorporate activities directly tied to learning outcomes.

- Help learners assess their own information needs and differentiate among sources of information, and help them develop skills to effectively identify, locate, and evaluate sources.
- Scale presentation content to the amount of time and space available.
- Design instruction to best meet the common learning characteristics of learners, including prior knowledge and experience, motivation to learn, cognitive abilities, and circumstances under which they will be learning.
- Integrate appropriate technology into instruction to support experiential and collaborative learning, as well as improve student receptiveness, comprehension, and retention of information.

Teaching Skills

- Create a learner-centered teaching environment by using active, collaborative, and other appropriate learning activities.
- Modify teaching methods and delivery to address different learning styles, language abilities, developmental skills, age groups, and the diverse needs of learners of all ages.
- Participate in constructive learner–teacher exchanges by encouraging participants to ask and answer questions, allowing adequate time, rephrasing questions, and asking probing or engaging questions.
- Modify teaching methods to match the group style and setting.
- In academic settings, encourage teaching faculty to participate in discussion during a class, link library instruction content to course content, and answer student questions.

Presentation Skills

- Make the best possible use of voice, eye contact, and gestures to keep class lively and students engaged.
- Present instructional content in diverse ways (written, oral, visual, online, video), and select appropriate delivery methods according to participant needs.
- Make smooth transitions between technological tools, if used.
- Seek to clarify confusing terminology, avoid excessive jargon, and use vocabulary appropriate for the level of those you are teaching.
- Practice or refine instruction content as necessary to achieve familiarity and confidence with a planned presentation.
- Reflect on practice to improve teaching skills and acquire new knowledge of teaching methods and learning theories.
- Share teaching skills and knowledge with other instructional staff.

Communication Skills

- Maintain awareness of the communication needs of different learning styles, and adjust your communication style and methods accordingly.
- Lead or facilitate discussion of controversial or unexpected issues in a skillful, non-judgmental manner that helps attendees learn.

- Use common communication technologies to provide assistance to learners inside and outside the learning environment.
- Request feedback from peers on instruction-related communication skills and use it for self-improvement.

Creating lessons, speaking to a group, managing activities, meeting learners for the first time—all create anxiety in the instructor. Procedures for addressing these issues and planning for effective instruction will alleviate many of these concerns. The success of the training effort depends on the effective use of your innate abilities, coupled with a systematic approach to developing and implementing instruction.

The instructor succeeds or fails in the learning environment. Here everything comes together, and it becomes apparent whether you are fully prepared and capable of carrying out the instructional task. It is not enough to be effective in lesson presentation but not prepared to work effectively with your learners. Alternatively, to be effective with your learners but not prepared to present the material is also unsatisfactory. You must be prepared and able, with an extensive array of skills and knowledge. These include knowledge of the instructional content; skill at efficiently presenting the material through the appropriate instructional media; awareness of each learner's needs and best learning style; basic understanding of learning theory for children and adults; and effective use of interpersonal skills when addressing a broad spectrum of learner performance, attitudes, skill levels, and interests.

Creating Instruction

The most effective instructors are good planners, especially of those skills involved in creating lessons and learning activities. Lesson plans are organized to provide regular opportunities for learners to actively practice, perform, and receive feedback on all required skills. Being able to develop an effective plan format is a core skill for all who teach.

Planning the Lesson

The goal of the lesson plan that you develop is to guide you in organizing your material and yourself to help your learners achieve intended outcomes. Whether your plan fits a particular format is not as relevant as whether it actually describes what you want your learners to achieve and what you have determined is the best means to attain that outcome. Here are some general tips:

- Delivery of material must be sequenced from simple to complex.
- Having clear and easily understood goals and objectives that take the learner along a path where the material is logically presented, explored, and then reinforced will help to avoid learner confusion.
- As learners experience achievement, they are cognitively ready to assume greater challenges in the learning process.
- Students need an accountable learning design and a teacher who is able to provide the necessary sequence and reinforcement of learning tasks, such as introducing concepts, explaining them, demonstrating them, and allowing learners to practice them.
- Learners are able to experience steady and progressive acquisition of skills through assisted and guided practice. Their accomplishments are then reinforced.

- Trust, mutual assistance, willingness to participate, and learning reinforcement all take place with each component, contributing to the learning environment in a positive way.
- Learners enhance their understanding of new knowledge when they have time to apply it, practice their newly acquired skills and attitudes, and then reflect on what they have just done based on their success and its applicability to their needs.
- It is conducive when teaching adults to inquire from them what their learning needs and desires are and how they are most comfortable in learning (e.g., learning styles must be taken into account).
- Learners need help in gaining new or enhanced skills and knowledge, with applicability to their immediate life needs.

Designing the Instruction

Course quality depends on the success of two activities: design and implementation. To design a learning session, you must state goals and plan activities to meet those goals. The instructor should construct his or her lesson plan with organization in mind. Facts and information should build on one another, in a logical manner, and according to some scheme that goes from easy to more complex concepts. In this way, students are able to grasp ideas, information, and concepts in a manner that is not confusing or overwhelming.

For our purposes, the lesson is divided into four general categories.

Preparation

Initiate any necessary preprogram work and program planning. Identify the knowledge and skills level of the trainees/learners at the start of the instruction.

Presentation

Provide training and learning resources to enable learners to comprehend within the objectives of the program and the learners' own objectives.

Application

Monitor the learning, and provide formative assessment as the program progresses, with a variety of user interactions, knowledge checks, and review activities to ensure learner engagement and comprehension.

Evaluation

At the end of the program, assess the learning levels achieved by participants via evaluation methods. Ensure that learners produce an action plan to reinforce, practice, and implement learning.

See chapter 5 for specifics of implementing workshops and chapter 6 for more about online instruction.

Step-by-Step Plan

This more detailed plan will help you create your lesson. Just follow these steps.

Step 1: Plan the Lesson

To plan instruction, an instructor librarian needs information. The instructor derives that information by taking into account the relevant developmental characteristics of the learners; the specific subject content; the available resources, including time, space, and materials; and the instructional methods, such as direct teaching, discussion, cooperative learning, and more that will work best in the defined situation. The goal is to attain a particular objective through a series of activities. At a minimum, the lesson plan should include the objective, a list of any required resources and materials, the instructional activities, and a description of how the learning objective will be measured.

A number of potential differences among learners will influence their ability to learn—their interaction with others, the materials, and their surroundings. Review figure 3.1 as you plan your instruction.

Assess the audience for instruction:

1. Assess personal skills, learner styles, interests, abilities, previous knowledge, strengths, and weak areas.
2. Analyze the organization in which instruction occurs: align philosophy, goals, and rules.
3. Determine learning outcomes: what will the learner know, feel, or be able to do at the end of instruction.
4. Identify content essential to achieve goals and satisfy learner needs.
5. Select methods, strategies, and resources appropriate for goals, learners, and content.
6. Determine how you will assess goal attainment and provide learner feedback.
7. Make a tentative plan with assigned times for each activity.

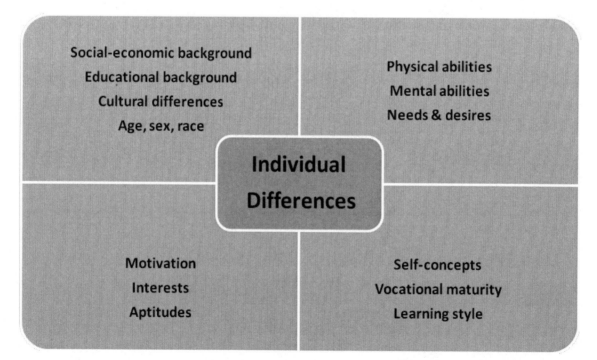

Figure 3.1. Learners' individual differences.

Step 2: Write Objectives

Objectives are important to select and design instructional content, materials, or methods and have a sound basis by which success can be measured. Defining your objectives for training is a critical step in the whole development process. Why? Without a training objective, instructors do not know exactly what it is to be taught, and learners do not know what they are to learn. By clearly stating the results that learners are to accomplish, instructor librarians can identify whether students have gained the appropriate skills and knowledge. Objectives should be stated before instruction because they provide students with the means to organize their efforts toward accomplishing the desired behaviors. A training objective contains a task (what is to be learned), a condition (how well it is to be performed), and a standard (under what conditions it is to be performed; see figure 3.2).

Learning objectives include four characteristics that help an objective communicate its intent:

Audience—Who will be doing the behavior?

Behavior/performance—What should the learner be able to do?

Condition—Under what conditions do you want the learner to be able to do it?

Degree—How well must it be done? Criteria might be speed, accuracy, or quality.

Objectives may encompass three areas: cognitive, psychomotor, and affective. Action verbs help to align objectives to an observable behavior, as in the following examples:

Cognitive: The learner will be able to identify five characteristics of a good job resume.

Psychomotor: The learner will be able to write an effective search strategy.

Affective: The learner will be able to reply appropriately to questions in an interview.

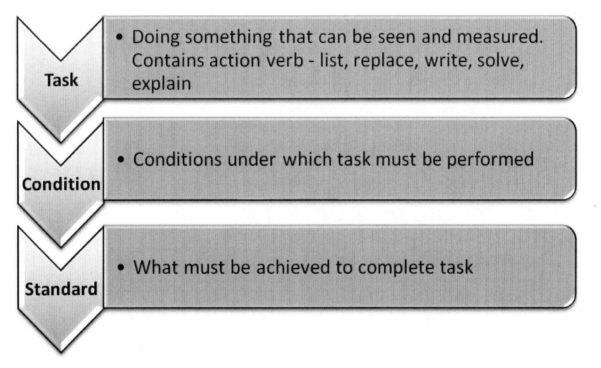

Task
- Doing something that can be seen and measured. Contains action verb - list, replace, write, solve, explain

Condition
- Conditions under which task must be performed

Standard
- What must be achieved to complete task

Figure 3.2. Writing objectives.

Objectives are concrete, precise, narrow, and tangible, and they can be validated. Goals, however, are broad, abstract, and intangible, and they cannot be validated; they are general intentions.

Step 3: Get Learners Connected

Whether the instruction is face-to-face or online, an important part is to gain the interest of the participants. If they are attentive, they will be more motivated to learn and absorb the content. Start by making connections with their prior learning and individual learning goals and by facilitating connections among themselves. Try one or more of these activities:

- Do a quick-write, where learners each write a sentence describing what they want to learn and then tell the group what they wrote.
- Have participants introduce themselves to one other person and tell that person three facts that they already know about the topic of the lesson.
- Have learners read the list of learning objectives, circle the one that is most important to them, and then tell the group which they circled and why.
- For online instruction, poll your users, ask questions in the chat box, or have learners identify their location on a world map so that they get to know one another.

Note: Put the welcome, introductions, announcements, learning objectives, and anything else after the connection activity.

Step 4: Chunk, Show, and Tell the Content

Now is the time to take out your bag of tricks containing a variety of activities that will actively involve participants in the material they are to learn. Here are some ideas to get you started:

- Begin with a story, current event, historical development, or statement of fact.
- Include examples to aid student understanding.
- Use personal experiences to add realism and practicality.
- Ask oral questions to elicit class involvement and check prior knowledge.
- Use activities to involve students and perform specific behaviors.
- Use transitions to signal to students that the lesson is progressing to a new point.

As you decide on beginning activities, note the following:

- Provide content in small "chunks" of ten- to twenty-minute segments. Insert quick one-minute activities between longer content segments.
- Use visual aids, and tell stories to teach content (e.g., photos, props, icons, cartoons, videos, graphics, demonstrations, and skits). Telling also includes case studies, analogies, and metaphors.
- Create graphic organizers for learners to use to take notes See figure 3.3 for an example of a graphic to use for problem solving.
- Follow each content chunk with a one-minute review. While the instruction session is taking place, formative assessment can help determine whether students

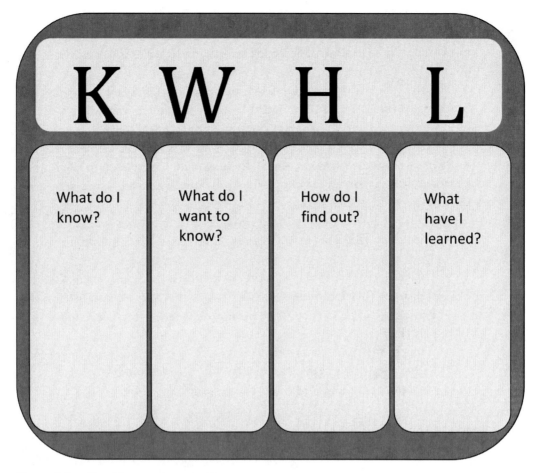

Figure 3.3. Graphic organizer template.

are mastering concepts. Instructors can also modify teaching methods and content during the session based on information solicited from participants.

Finally, conduct a formative assessment activity. Have students do the following:

- Write and share a one-sentence summary of the main ideas presented so far.
- Pair up and ask each other a content-related question, then discuss the answers.
- Write a content-related question on an index card, then pass the card to another learner, who writes the answer. Discuss later with the group.

Step 5: Involve Learners

Instructors must invite learners to actively participate in the learning process. This can be accomplished using small groups, team exercises, presentations, discussion groups, and numerous other techniques. All lesson plans should contain several activities where the learner is involved in some manner. It is fine to deliver information as an instructor, but there should also be methods and techniques for learner involvement throughout the process. Providing information and demonstration, followed by practice that is evaluated and then repeated, enhances learning.

For example, if you are teaching a small group at your local public library how to sign up and use Facebook, you might give a brief description or ask patrons what they know about social media and why they are interested in using Facebook. This provides information and emphasizes what learners want to take away from the learning. The instructor might model how to create a Facebook account and have users set up their own accounts on the library computers.

At that point, the instructor can demonstrate how to "friend" a member of the group, and users can then friend one another. This gives learners immediate reinforcement on what they learned. Finally, students can list what they plan to gain from using Facebook. The instructor can set some goals, such as visiting a friend's Facebook page, adding friends to their pages, and writing messages. These activities require learners to use what they learned right away. If they know that they will not use the program in the near future, the learning impact is diminished.

Activities that you choose will depend on the structure of your instruction. Chapter 4 provides more on different types of learning structure. Here are some samples:

- Divide learners into pairs or groups of three, and have them take turns either explaining concepts or demonstrating skills that they learned in the class.
- Have groups choose a concept or skill to demonstrate or explain to the rest of the participants.
- Groups of learners create and act out a skit that demonstrates a concept or skill.
- In pairs, learners role-play a situation, such as a job interview.
- Use online breakout rooms to work in teams.

Step 6: Create Handouts

Handouts are an important part of training sessions. They reinforce what is taught during the session, and they provide a means to review material. Handouts can also reduce the need to take notes. For those who cannot attend the training, handouts can be sent to them.

The appearance of the handout is also critical to its success: Streamline the content and avoid clutter. Make it visually pleasing, with graphics and illustrations to emphasize main points. Vary the font size to identify main points and subpoints. If you are using PowerPoint slides, you may want to create miniature copies of the visuals. Attendees can then add notes on the slides. The handouts may be in Microsoft Word, but some presenters may prefer to post Adobe PDFs. All should be printable and downloadable.

Before they present their training programs, instructors typically provide electronic copies of the handouts they will be using. If it is a live session, they should err on the side of having too many. It is often a good idea to create a one-page summary of the library's training program so that participants will have immediate access to the handouts when they return to their libraries.

Step 7: Evaluate the Learning with an Action Plan

Different types of evaluation can occur during your instructional session. Formative evaluation and ongoing assessment during a workshop or class are important components. At the end of the session, a summative assessment can provide valuable insight into what students learned, how they felt about the instruction, and if the instructor needs to modify the lesson plan.

You will want to think about incorporating the following as part of your evaluation:

- Initiate any necessary preprogram work and planning.
- Identify the knowledge and skills level of the trainees or learners at the start of the instruction.
- Provide training and learning resources to enable the learners to comprehend within the objectives of the lesson and the learners' own objectives.
- Monitor the learning as the session progresses with a variety of user interactions, knowledge checks, and review activities to ensure learner engagement.
- At the end of the session, assess learning levels achieved via evaluation methods. These can take various forms, some of which you will see in examples in subsequent chapters.
- Ensure that learners produce an action plan to reinforce, practice, and implement learning. The action plan is a commitment by learners to use what they have learned or practiced. It allows them time to evaluate what they have learned and think about how it applies to their work.

Although the principal role of the participants in instruction is to learn, they must also be involved in the evaluation process. This is essential since, without their comments, much of the evaluation could not occur. Make sure that trainees understand the importance of their input—exactly what and why they are asked to be involved (see handout 3.1 for a sample).

With the ever-changing nature of the library's work, the library staff need fresh and innovative training opportunities to stay current and continue to meet the needs of their patrons. Managing staff training involves assessment of training needs, planning and evaluating staff development, and keeping on top of all the learning methods and formats available. Whether conducting training face-to-face or online, through a blend of both,

EVALUATION MODEL

Used over the years by numbers of instructional designers, Kirkpatrick's model (1994) helps evaluate the effectiveness of a training program. The evaluation model, originally divided into four levels, was created to measure learners'

Reaction—what learners thought and felt about the training

Learning—their resulting increase in knowledge or capability

Behavior—the extent of their behavior and capability improvement and implementation and application of what they learned

Results—the effects on the business or environment resulting from the learners' performances

This model has changed somewhat for training in the business community. The revised model is now being used for planning and evaluation.

HANDOUT 3.1. Sample Training and Learning Evaluation Form

Directions: Answer these questions following the training.

Questions	Answers
To what extent were the identified training needs achieved by the program?	
To what extent were the learners' objectives obtained?	
What specifically did you learn or were you reminded of?	
What commitment have you made about the learning that you are going to implement on your return to work?	
What do you intend to do with the information you gained or skills you developed?	
Were the training program handouts practical, adaptable, and suitable for sharing with colleagues?	

Directions: Answer the following questions within two weeks of returning to work.

Questions	Answers
How successful were you in implementing your action plans?	
To what extent were you supported in this by your managers?	
To what extent has the action listed above achieved a return on investment for the organization—in terms of identified objectives, satisfaction or, where possible, a monetary assessment?	

or as augmented with social media tools, managing staff learning can be the basis for a transformative and accessible learning organization for all.

◎ Key Points: Taking an Action Approach

Action learning is defined as an approach to working with, and developing people, which uses work on a real project or problem as the way to learn. Participants work in small groups or teams to take action to complete their project or solve a problem, and learn how to learn from that action. A learning facilitator works with the group in order to help them learn how to balance their work, with the learning from that work. (O'Neil and Lamm 2000, 44)

The teaching–learning process is dynamic, interactive, and cooperative. Each person participating has some responsibility for its success or failure. Teams encourage a collective effort in accomplishing learning objectives and thereby enhance the overall learning process. When a team has been given the responsibility of carrying out some desired action or completing specific tasks, learning is enhanced. Those composing a team must determine a course of action, work out assignments, find solutions to problems, learn to mediate, determine alternative actions, as well as other tasks. Using effective classroom training techniques, promoting active learning, adapting instruction to meet the needs of learners, and encouraging individual practice all increase learning. See table 3.1 for instructional techniques and table 3.2 for additional links to websites on information covered in this chapter.

Table 3.1. Instructional Techniques

COMPETENCY	SKILLS/KNOWLEDGE
Practice effective training techniques	• Explain the goals and objectives of the class • Present ideas clearly • Use a variety of approaches to accommodate learning styles • Actively listen to learner input
Promote active learning in the classroom	• Provide examples • Allow time for question and answer • Accommodate various learning styles by using handouts, hands-on learning, and small group work
Receive feedback from learners and respond by adapting instruction to meet their needs	• Check in with learners to ensure that they are understanding concepts • Adapt activities based on individual learning preferences, level of skill, and level of support needed • Allow learners time to evaluate the session and the effectiveness of the trainer
Demonstrate classroom management techniques	• Set ground rules and boundaries in the training • Be prepared to deal with difficult situations
Encourage learners to practice outside of the session	• Offer ideas and techniques for independent practice • Share tutorials and other resources for learners' self-paced learning

Table 3.2. URLs for Chapter 3

DESCRIPTION	URL
Lesson plans for public libraries	http://www.webjunction.org/documents/webjunction/Creating_Lesson_Plans_for_Teaching_the_Public.html
Evaluating websites lesson plan	http://www.webjunction.org/documents/webjunction/Evaluating_Web_Sites_Lesson_Plan.html
Refining web searches lesson plan	http://www.webjunction.org/documents/webjunction/Beyond_the_Basics_045_Refining_Web_Searches.html
Tips on designing training, including videos	http://www.bowperson.com/articles.htm
Training delivery methods	http://www.techsoupforlibraries.org/blog/beyond-lecture-training-delivery-methods

EXERCISES: Now You Try It . . .

To reinforce what you learned about lesson planning and delivering instruction, try the following.

1. Identify one topic that would meet your patrons' needs (e.g., evaluating a website, interviewing for a job, writing a resume, performing a search), and write a lesson plan following the model in this chapter.
   a. Assess the audience, including adult versus youth and prior knowledge on the subject, and create a formative evaluation.
   b. Complete the lesson plan template. Use handout 3.2 or a format of your own design.
   c. Create a handout (or handouts) to be used with this lesson.
   d. Plan at least three activities to use during the lesson.
   e. Create a summative evaluation form and a learner self-evaluation form.
   f. Develop a follow-up evaluation to determine if and how training participants used the training they received—and, if they did not use the training, why not.
2. Deliver the lesson. Immediately following, take notes on the session.
3. Based on the instruction, create and complete an assessment of your lesson and performance: What went well? What would you change and how? Did anything occur that you had not anticipated? If so, what and how would you change your plan?

Lesson title	
General plan	
Purpose	
Goal	
Objectives	
Outline steps or sequence of content	
Activities to guide the learner	
Activities to use for practice	
Evaluation	
Follow-up	

⊚ References

Association of College and Research Libraries. 2007. *Standards for Proficiencies for Instruction Librarians and Coordinators.* Chicago: American Library Association. http://www.ala.org/acrl/standards/guidelinesinstruction.

Baker, Jean M. 2010, March 3. "Peer Coaching for Teaching and Learning." *Essential Educator Newsletter.* http://essentialeducator.org/?p=688.

Hoffman, Judy, John Carlo Bertot, and Denise M. Davis. 2012. "Libraries Connect Communities: Public Library Funding and Technology Access Study 2011–2012." *American Libraries,* June, digital supplement. http://viewer.zmags.com/publication/4673a369.

Kirkpatrick, D. L. 1994. *Evaluating Training Programs.* San Francisco: Berrett-Koehler.

McKinney, Kathleen. 2010. *Active Learning.* Normal, IL: Center for Teaching, Learning & Technology.

O'Neil, J., and S. L. Lamm. 2000, fall. "*Working as a Learning Coach Team in Action Learning.*" *New Directions for Adult and Continuing Education* 87:43–52.

⊚ Further Reading

Braxton, J. M., W. A. Jones, A. S. Hirschy, and H. V. Hartley III. 2008. "The Role of Active Learning in College Persistence." *New Directions for Teaching and Learning* 115:71–83.

Clark, R. E. 2003. "What Works in Distance Learning: Instructional Strategies." In *What Works in Distance Learning,* edited by H. F. O'Neil, 13–31. Los Angeles: Center for the Study of Evaluation.

Dembo, M., and L. G. Young. 2003. "What Works in Distance Education: Learning Strategies." In *What Works in Distance Education,* edited by H. F. O'Neil, 13–31. Los Angeles: Center for the Study of Evaluation.

Dunaway, Michelle Kathleen, and Michael Teague Orblych. 2011. "Formative Assessment: Transforming Information Literacy Instruction." *Reference Services Review* 39 (1): 24–41.

Houle, C. O. 1972. *The Design of Education.* San Francisco: Jossey-Bass.

Merriam, S. B. 2001. "Andragogy and Self-Directed Learning: Pillars of Adult Learning Theory." *New Directions for Adult and Continuing Education* 89:3–14.

Miller, Carolyn, Kristen Purcell, and Lee Rainie. 2011. *Reading Habits in Different Communities.* Washington, DC: Pew Internet & American Life Project. http://libraries.pewinternet.org/2012/12/20/reading-habits-in-different-communities/.

Salas, Eduardo. 2009. "Patient Safety Training Evaluations: Reflections on Level 4 and More." Slide presentation (text version) from the annual conference of the Agency for Healthcare Research and Quality, September, Rockville, MD. http://www.ahrq.gov/about/annualconf09/salas.htm.

University of North Carolina, Center for Faculty Excellence. 2009. "Classroom Activities for Active Learning." http://cfe.unc.edu/pdfs/FYC2.pdf.

Types of Instruction

INSTRUCTING PATRONS and offering information literacy training has become the role of librarians, and it continues to grow in the academic library as well as public and special libraries. Today's librarians are faced with the need to develop a more focused set of skills to teach effectively in their libraries. At the same time, many libraries are struggling to offer meaningful training and professional development to improve instruction, especially without a set of established standards for what constitutes a good teacher.

The Association of College and Research Libraries is the source that the higher education community looks to for standards and guidelines on academic libraries. The association creates standards and guidelines to help libraries, academic institutions, and accrediting agencies understand the components of an excellent library. These standards, guidelines, and model statements are reviewed and updated by the membership on a regular basis.

Chapters 4–8 are intended to help instruction librarians define and gain the skills needed to be excellent teachers in library instruction programs and to foster collaborations necessary to create and improve information literacy programs and more. Each lesson provides a model that librarians can use to create a plan of instruction on different topics. For example, teaching how to evaluate information retrieved is only one part of becoming information literate. Librarians may want to create a series of lessons that include creating search statements, refining a search to obtain more relevant results, and identifying and learning about the library's databases and other sources. For academic librarians, these topics all relate to central standards created by the Association of College and Research Libraries.

Chapter 4 outlines different types and modes of instruction, delivery methods, and examples of each.

How to Design, Create, and Deliver Training

Libraries are being called upon for a variety of services, especially accessing and learning about technology. These skills are vital for many twenty-first-century jobs. How are libraries going to help these patrons? Every time someone asks you a question, your response is a form of training. Depending on whether individuals visit a public, academic, or special library, some will come alone wanting to learn how to access tax forms; others will need basic computer skills (e.g., searching the Internet, creating a Facebook account); and still others will desire instruction on locating information for a school project. Classes of students need advice on information literacy skills. No matter whether the instruction is one-to-one or to a small group or an entire class, the library must and can meet patrons' needs.

Identifying Instructional Types

As you consider programs and services that your library can deliver to support job seekers and entrepreneurs and increase patrons' financial and technological literacy, keep in mind the broader context of skills important in the twenty-first century. For each library response, think about preparing your patrons for the reality of continuous learning and about helping them to build the attitude and skills they need to know how to learn.

This chapter provides an overview of different types of learning and modes of delivering instruction, such as face-to-face, online, blended, and self-paced. Examples illustrate instruction in public, academic, and special libraries and offer ideas to help you create your own instruction. Chapters 5–8 review each mode of delivery in more depth. Also discussed is the importance of marketing library programs and reaching out through other sources of instruction.

First Principles of Instruction

As mentioned in previous chapters, instruction should employ active learning strategies and techniques that require learners to develop their critical thinking in concert with information literacy skills. Planning such active learning should be carried out collaboratively with faculty in academic libraries, with patrons in public libraries, and with management in special libraries to increase overall learner engagement and extend opportunities for a more reflective approach to information retrieval, evaluation, and use on a variety of topics. Ask yourself the questions that are part of Merrill's (2002) first principles of instruction, as preparation for creating your instruction.

Merrill's first principles identify learning activities that should be included in effective instruction: activation, demonstration, application, and integration. First principles can be found in some form in almost all the instructional design theories and models discussed in chapter 2, yet many appear in general form only and do not include all the stages listed here.

Problem Centered: Understand the Whole Task

- Does the instruction involve authentic real-world problems or tasks?
- In place of a formal objective, does the instruction show the learners the whole task they will be able to do or the whole problem they will be able to solve as a result of completing the instruction?
- Does the instruction teach the components of the problem or task and then help the learner use these components in solving the whole problem or doing the whole task?
- Does the instruction involve a progression of problems and not just a single application?

Activation: Decide Where to Start

- Does the instruction direct learners to recall, relate, describe, or apply prior knowledge from relevant past experience that can be used as a foundation for the new knowledge?
- If learners have limited prior experience, does the instruction provide relevant experience that can be used as a foundation for the new knowledge?
- Does the instruction help learners see its relevance and have confidence in their ability to acquire the knowledge and skill to be taught?
- Does the instruction provide or encourage the recall of a structure that can be used to organize the new knowledge?

Demonstration: Show Me Rather Than Tell Me

- Does the instruction demonstrate (i.e., show examples of) what is to be learned rather than merely tell information about what is to be learned?
- Are the demonstrations consistent with the content being taught?
- Are multiple representations included and explicitly compared?
- Are learners assisted in relating the new information to the structure that was recalled or provided?
- Are the media relevant to the content and used to enhance learning?

Application: Provide Opportunities for Doing

- Do learners have an opportunity to practice and apply their newly acquired knowledge or skill?
- Is the practice followed by corrective feedback and an indication of progress—that is, not just right–wrong feedback?

- Does the application or practice enable learners to access context-sensitive help or provide coaching when they are having difficulty solving the problem or doing the task? Is coaching gradually lessened with each subsequent task until learners are performing on their own?
- Does the instruction require learners to use their new knowledge or skill to solve a varied sequence of problems or complete a sequence of tasks?

Integration: Reflect and Obtain Feedback

- Does the instruction provide techniques that encourage learners to integrate (transfer) the new knowledge or skill into their everyday lives?
- Does the instruction provide an opportunity for learners to publicly demonstrate their new knowledge or skill?
- Does the instruction provide an opportunity for learners to reflect on, discuss, and defend their new knowledge or skill?
- Does the instruction provide an opportunity for learners to create, invent, or explore new and personal ways to use their new knowledge or skill?

Implementation: Perform the Task

- Does the instruction facilitate learner navigation through the learning task?
- Is the degree of learner control appropriate for the learning goals and your learners?
- Is collaboration used effectively?
- Is the instruction personalized?

Answering these questions will help you to determine what type of instruction best meets the needs of your audience (see figure 4.1).

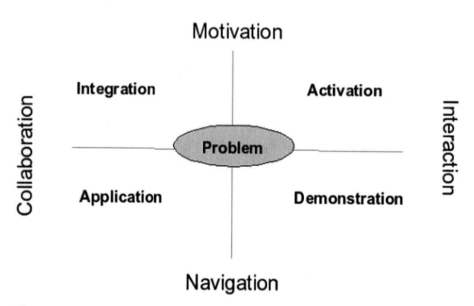

Figure 4.1. Principles to consider when creating instruction.

Types of Instruction

Instruction occurs in different modes and through a variety of strategies. The selected modes should be consistent with the goals of the instruction. Learning styles should be considered and multiple strategies incorporated whenever possible. Any method that an instruction librarian uses has advantages and disadvantages and so requires some preliminary preparation. Which instructional method is "right" for a particular occasion depends on many things—among them, the age and developmental level of the audience; what the patrons already know about the content; what they need to know to succeed with the lesson; the objectives of the lesson; the available people, time, space, and material resources; and the physical setting. There is no one right method for teaching a particular lesson, but there are some criteria that pertain to each that can help the instructor make the best decision possible.

Librarians and staff who are engaged in instructional activities are encouraged to participate in staff development opportunities related to improving and developing their expertise in this area. Methods of instruction mentioned here include direct instruction, learner-centered instruction, and independent learning.

Direct Instruction

Direct instruction is used to help library patrons learn concepts and skills. This teacher-centered approach includes instruction wherein the teacher's role is to present the information that is to be learned and direct the learning process of participants. There are various models of direct instruction, but all include similar steps: introduction and review, presentation of new information, guided practice, and independent practice. The instructor identifies the lesson objectives and takes the primary responsibility for guiding the instruction by explaining the information and modeling. This is followed by student practice. Examples of methods that fall into the teacher-centered approaches include lecture, discussion, and demonstration.

Lecture. The lecture is one of the most frequently used instructional methods in adult education. It is one-way, and there is little to no interaction with the students—for example, a PowerPoint presentation to convey content to the students. It assumes the librarian to be the expert, and it is an efficient way of disseminating information. Most educators agree that the purpose of lectures is to lay foundations as the students work through the subject, and good lecturers know their students and develop their lectures according to the students' needs. Most important, lectures are most effective when used in combination with other instructional strategies. Lectures can also be presented via audio or video over the Internet. Short online lectures provide enough information to serve as a basis for further reading, research, or other learning activities and still keep the attention of learners.

Discussion. Instructors often incorporate discussion into the lecture format. Discussion is the instructional strategy most favored by adult learners because it is interactive and encourages active, participatory learning. The discussion format encourages learners to analyze alternative ways of thinking and acting and assists learners in exploring their own experiences. Online discussion can take place via chat rooms or other video technology, such as Skype.

Demonstration. In a demonstration, the instruction librarian shows students or patrons how to do a task or perform a procedure, such as conduct a Google search or use the library catalog, without the audience doing anything. Involving students in demonstrations allows this method to be less passive.

Learner-Centered Instruction

Learner-centered approaches involve instruction where the teacher is a facilitator as learners construct their own understandings. Examples include project-based learning, problem-based learning, collaboration, cooperative learning, case study, forums, role-play, and learning by teaching. Some of these approaches can also be used in an independent learning environment.

Project-based learning. In project-based learning, projects begin with the end in mind. Through independent and interdependent learning, users conduct a detailed investigation of all issues and opinions within the problem. Life skills—including teamwork, time management, research, communication, and computing skills—are strengthened. In project-based learning, the primary goal is the learning. Patrons spend time learning by identifying what they need to know, finding it (from the library, Internet, colleagues, etc.), teaching one another, and then applying their new knowledge to the project.

Projects give students an opportunity to pursue their special interests, and they can be done individually or within groups, face-to-face or online. Using projects in a learning activity makes the learning more relevant to the learners. Products can be shared with others and critiqued, thus exposing learners to more viewpoints. Group projects can include simulations, role-playing studies, problem-solving exercises, group collaborative work, debates, small group discussion, and brainstorming.

Problem-based learning. In this approach learners use real-world problems as a context to not only acquire skills but also think critically and creatively while developing skills for solving problems. Students in small groups investigate and analyze problems/scenarios. Using a three-step process, they identify the facts in the problem/scenario, generate (uncriticized) ideas to determine what the problem is, and identify what they have to learn to test their hypotheses (ideas). The advantage of this approach is that it helps students become familiar with scientific reasoning and fills gaps in their knowledge bases so that they can use their newly acquired knowledge to refine or discard their ideas. In their small groups, they investigate real problems.

Collaboration and cooperative learning. Collaborative learning is the process of getting two or more students to work together to learn. Students work in small groups composed of participants with differing ability levels, and using a variety of learning activities, they master material developed by an instructor or construct knowledge on substantive issues. Each team member is responsible for learning what is taught and for helping teammates learn. Collaboration is a necessary technique to promote cognitive development, self-esteem, and positive student–student relationships. Through cooperative learning, students work collaboratively toward a common goal or task, and tasks are shared equally among a heterogeneous group.

Case study. A case study is a teaching strategy that requires learners to draw on their past experiences; it is participatory and has action components that are links to future experience. The key to a successful case study is the selection of an appropriate problem situation, which is relevant to the interests and experience level of learners and to the concepts being taught. One advantage of using the case method is that it emphasizes practical thinking; it assists learners in first identifying principles after examining the facts of the case and then applying those principles to new situations. In the online environment, case studies can be presented on webpages and discussed in conferencing groups. Cases can be developed by class groups as collaborative projects.

Case studies present students with real-life problems and enable them to apply what they learned in the classroom to life situations. Cases also encourage students to develop logical problem-solving skills and, if used in teams, group interaction skills. Students define problems, analyze possible actions, and provide solutions with a rationale for their choices.

Forums. The forum is an open discussion carried on by one or more resource people and an entire group. The moderator guides the discussion, and the audience raises and discusses issues, makes comments, offers information, and asks questions of the resource person and one another. There are two variations of the forum: the panel and the symposium. The panel is usually a group of three to six people who sit in the presence of an audience and have a purposeful conversation on a topic in which they have specialized knowledge. The symposium is more formal in that experts present insights on a subject, followed by questions. Because the online environment facilitates group communication, it is ideal for the types of information exchange typical in forums.

Role-play. In a role-play, a problem is identified, acted out, and discussed. The role-play process provides students with an opportunity to explore their feelings, gain insight about their attitudes, and increase their problem-solving skills. For example, in a public library, two children might make up a dialogue between two characters from a book and perform it to the rest of their library book group.

Learning by teaching. This method allows students to prepare and teach lessons or parts of lessons. Students not only convey content but also choose their methods and approaches to teach others the subject. An adult learner with specific skills in accounting can demonstrate how a group can find tax information online and can point out forms to select.

Independent Learning

Self-directed learning is initiated and directed by the learner and can include self-paced, self-directed, and individualized learning as well as self-instruction. Whatever terminology is used, self-directed learning places the responsibility for learning directly on the learner. The independent learner is one who is more involved and active within the learning process. Online learning supports the self-directed learner in pursuing individualized, self-paced instructional activities. With this method, a student-centered learning environment is created where inquiry is the norm, problem solving becomes the focus, and thinking critically is part of the process.

Various methods discussed under learner-centered instruction, such as problem- and inquiry-based learning, can be used to facilitate independent learning. Students learn through an inductive or inquiry approach in which they are encouraged and enabled to find answers for themselves. Inquiry-based learning follows a five-step approach:

Engage—teachers gain students' interest in the topic but do not explicitly teach the topic.

Explore—students acquire knowledge themselves, through questioning and experimenting.

Explain—students explain their learning, with the teacher providing guidance.

Elaborate—students use the knowledge learned and apply it in a new context.

Evaluate—teachers evaluate students' learning.

Independent or autonomous learners take full responsibility for their own learning. In an online learning environment where teachers can be at a distance and parent support can be limited, the skill of independent learning is highly helpful. You can help your student become more independent by encouraging the above characteristics.

◉ Modes to Deliver Instruction

Depending on the type of library, instruction can be very different. Face-to-face training methods are the most common, but this is changing. In higher education, a lecture format has been often used, especially in large classes. More learning-centered instruction, such as problem based, collaboration, and project based, is used in classes with smaller enrollment so that students learn to work together to solve problems, whereas patrons in a special library may want to explore inquiry-based and self-directed learning so that they can work independently.

Academic librarians have emphasized instruction offering classroom training in conjunction with faculty or sessions in the library. Public librarians use a combination of information and guidance, such as individual programs or a series of courses on finding business, career, genealogical, local history, parenting, or other information of interest to many people. In contrast, special librarians provide the information directly, not usually in the form of citations, but in the form of reports and recommendations. Much instruction that does occur in special libraries is individualized, although they do conduct some workshops, small group instruction, and sessions with guest speakers, especially database vendors. All libraries now use indirect instruction in the form of self-paced materials—LibGuides, pathfinders, search aids, videos, and more.

Face-to-Face Training

Face-to-face interactive training (e.g., small group work, one-to-one, workshop, class) is the most common instructional mode. However, it is not the answer to every training need, and it can be provided through a variety of methods (see chapter 5 for more details on strategies).

Instructional strategies are most effective when employed to meet particular learning goals and objectives. Begin by asking and answering this key question: What are the major learning goals and objectives for the instruction that you plan to create? Once these have been identified and clearly articulated, you can then address the question of which learning strategies, activities, and experiences to employ.

Classroom Instruction

Primarily designed for academic libraries, classroom instruction can be offered by a librarian in many forms:

- working with a professor and students in a seminar or discussion setting or brainstorming research topics, methods, and resources;
- making a short visit to a classroom for introduction and explanation of how a librarian can help students;
- leading a session in an e-library classroom for hands-on experience with library resources;

- going to a large lecture hall and working with a faculty member leading discussion and group exercises;
- collaborating with a faculty member during the course development phase, helping to plan the course syllabus and research exercises;
- embedding in the classroom, working regularly with the students and coteaching the course; and
- teaching a one-credit directed-study library course for, say, chemistry graduate students.

Face-to-face training is most effective for longer training sessions. For each classroom session, librarians are encouraged to develop student learning outcomes and describe how students will act and think differently as a result of successfully completing a course. The librarian focuses on what the student will be able to do, rather than on what content to cover. Well-defined learning outcomes specify actions by students that are measurable, observable, and completed by the students themselves.

With the objectives in mind, instruction librarians can then engage the pedagogical methods that best meet the student learning outcomes that they and the faculty member set for their students. Pedagogies that are frequently employed include the following:

Active learning—employs a variety of approaches to place the primary responsibility of creating and applying knowledge on the students themselves. It puts the student at the center of the learning process, making him or her a partner in discovery, not a passive receiver of information. Active learning requires students to interact with and integrate course material by reading, writing, discussing, problem solving, investigating, reflecting, and engaging in higher-order thinking tasks, such as analysis, synthesis, evaluation, and creation.

Informed learning—combines the act of learning to use information and learning about a subject. To facilitate informed learning, an instructor would design a learning scenario so that students are asked to learn to use information, such as learning general or disciplinary information practices, while also learning subject content.

Peer-led discussions—students have opportunities to talk about their ideas and respond to those of others.

Problem-based learning—student-centered pedagogy in which students learn about a subject in the context of complex, multifaceted, realistic problems. Working in groups, students identify what they already know, what they need to know, and how and where to access new information that may lead to a resolution of the problem. The instructor assumes the role of facilitator, who provides appropriate support and modeling of the process while monitoring the learning.

Academic instruction librarians often engage with faculty in academic programs, including

- general education core requirements,
- research methods courses in disciplinary majors,
- writing intensive and capstone courses,
- undergraduate research experiences and internships,
- distance education, and
- experiential service learning courses.

Examples illustrate face-to-face classroom courses being offered on a range of topics in different subject areas.

Example 1: West Virginia University Libraries. Academic libraries add value to the teaching and learning missions of their universities through information literacy instruction. The West Virginia University Libraries, for example, already offer expert research instruction across many disciplines to provide students and others with the skills and knowledge to identify, find, and evaluate information. Introduction to Library Research is a one-credit course that reaches over eight hundred first-year through senior students each year, and the Information Literacy Course Enhancement Program has taught more than eleven hundred students since 2010. Through collaboration with teaching faculty, librarians help to integrate information literacy into the curriculum. Together, faculty and librarians design exercises and assignments to assist students in practicing research-based skills. Courses in information literacy are also designed for faculty (for more about West Virginia's program, see https://www.libraries.wvu.edu/instruction/infolit/plan/plan).

Example 2: Kimbel Library Services, Coastal Carolina University. Two examples show the success of Kimbel Library Services at Coastal Carolina University.

Ryan Shelley is a teacher of first-year composition in the English department at Coastal Carolina University. He helps incoming students become more sophisticated researchers. He comments that Kimbel provides the resources and services to help him better meet the research needs of his writing students. The instruction sessions give students guided, hands-on experience with effective search strategies for navigating through the wealth of materials the library has to offer (see http://www.coastal.edu/library/?page=pageContent/testimonials/shelley.html).

Mary Kate Powell teaches in the Department of Health Promotion at Coastal Carolina University. She has scheduled her Community Health Education Methods class for library instruction with two librarians so that the students are informed on what resources are available for their research projects and how to use the tools. Mary Kate states, "I was very impressed with the format of the training because the library staff not only explained the information and provided demonstrations, but they challenged my students to be resourceful and apply their knowledge to complete a series of activities right there in the computer lab" (see http://www.coastal.edu/library/?page=pageContent/testimonials/powell.html).

Example 3: New York University Libraries. New York University Libraries schedule general classes on RefWorks Basics, EndNote Basics, Zotera, and citation tracking, as well as special interest sessions for business students (learn more about their program at https://webapps.library.nyu.edu/classes/#managing-your-research-and-bibliographies-with-refworks).

Workshops

Workshops held in the library can be based on a variety of subjects, such as using Google, EndNote, or RefWorks and understanding copyright. Some workshops may also be created to meet a specific department's needs, such as teaching with archives, using multimedia in the classroom, and information literacy for graduate students.

The following workshop examples illustrate some of these uses.

Example 1: Olin and Uris Libraries, Cornell University. The goal of Olin and Uris Libraries at Cornell University is to meet the needs of teaching faculty in educating their students on how to conduct library research while promoting information literacy. Opportunities include course-related instruction to students at all levels. Library instructors work closely with the first-year writing program, as well as upper-level undergraduate and graduate courses. Class sessions are held in the library's hands-on instructional facility. The session consists of an overview of the library system and explains library research methodology. A hands-on experience with the Cornell Library Catalog and appropriate networked resources is part of the training. Workshops are also given on creating webpages, using citation management with RefWorks software, conducting library research, and information management (see more on the Cornell Libraries at http://olin-uris.library.cornell.edu/content/instruction).

Example 2: Chicago Public Library. The Chicago Public Library and its outreach locations offer numerous workshops, from croquet to basic computer skills, as well as job-preparedness workshops on how to write a resume, search for a job online, complete an online job application, and interview for a job.

One-on-One Interactive Instruction

Subject librarians and reference staff view every one-on-one consultation with a patron as a teaching moment. They provide one-on-one instruction in individually scheduled consultations as well as via e-mail, phone, text, and walk-up interactions at the library service desk. Topics include writing assistance, copyright issues, and citation management tools, to name a few.

Many public, academic and special libraries focus on one-on-one instruction, both face-to-face and online.

Example 1: Cornell University's one-on-one sources. Cornell's Ask a Librarian provides one-on-one instruction through a variety of sources: instant messaging, mobile, reference consultation appointments, 24/7 chat, e-mail, text, and phone. The librarian answers questions on search, course work, research, library services, and special requests.

Example 2: Brooklyn Public Library's Book a Librarian. Book a Librarian at Brooklyn Public Library offers half-hour personal assistance on topics such as researching an assignment; finding business, government, or medical information; searching for an ancestor; or using the library's databases. The business library provides business and finance consultations, as well as instruction in job searching and resume editing (learn more at http://bplsite.brooklynpubliclibrary.org/locations/business.html).

Small Group Work

In small groups, learners can discuss content, share ideas, and solve problems. They can present their ideas as well as consider those of others. In this way, they are exposed to a variety of viewpoints on a given subject.

- A discussion group allows learners to reflect on a subject under discussion and present their views. Book clubs for adults, teens, and children usually follow this format with a facilitator.
- Role-play involves re-creating a situation relating to a real-world problem in which participants act out various roles. This promotes an understanding of other people's positions and their attitudes, as well as the procedures that might be used for diagnosing and solving problems. Role-play can simulate real-life group work situations, such as applying for a job.
- Games requiring two or more groups to compete while attempting to meet a set of objectives are another form of small group learning requiring decision making. Most instructional games reflect typical life situations.

Note: Small groups can also be created in online learning environments through breakout rooms. These groups can work independently while still having access to an instructor. More about small online groups is provided in chapter 7.

The following examples demonstrate several small group activities for libraries and might provide ideas for yours.

Example 1: Brooklyn Public Library. Brooklyn Public Library Learning Centers provide a free innovative literacy program for beginning adult readers and writers at a pre-GED level. Through books, technology, and small group instruction, adults build the skills needed to meet their personal, educational, and employment goals (learn more about the program at http://bplsite.brooklynpubliclibrary.org/only-bpl/adult-literacy.html).

Example 2: Vanderbilt University Law School. The Vanderbilt University Law School relies on law librarians to share their expertise in how to "find the law." Instruction librarians initiate new students into the wide, changing world of legal information. Each librarian has close contact with a small group of students, who learn important research skills while forming close relationships with their instructors. Students also learn to view librarians not only as mentors and teachers but as information resources. Teaching legal research further forces instructors to keep current with legal trends, as well as changes in legal publishing and legal information resources. As research instructors, instruction librarians in the legal writing course lecture, develop sample exercises, and create weekly graded assignments (read about this program at http://www.library.vanderbilt.edu/mosaic/role.shtml).

Example 3: Fast Forward New Mexico. Fast Forward New Mexico is a grant-funded program awarded to the New Mexico State Library. Its purpose is to bring free computer and Internet training, information, and broadband awareness to rural, Hispanic, and Native American populations. Public libraries hold free classes on using the Internet for business (increasing sales, social media marketing), and they offer a basic computer skills series. More than thirty-five hundred patrons have completed Fast Forward New Mexico classes (review their website at http://www.fastforwardnm.org).

Online Instruction

Online instruction allows patrons to get help any time they need it from wherever they are. Web-based training is most effective for short training sessions, often focused on technology applications. These online programs may cost more initially than face-to-face programs, but the long-term costs are often considerably less because the online programs can be offered multiple times. Furthermore, it is appropriate to use online courses to train people to use online resources. The examples that follow demonstrate the different ways that libraries are using online learning.

Example 1: Online Degree

The master of library and information science program at the San José State University School of Library and Information Science, with all instruction completed online, prepares students for careers as information professionals who work in a myriad of information environments. Students interact with peers and instructors through web conferencing, social networking platforms, a web-based learning management system, and immersive environments. Most course content is delivered asynchronously—giving students the freedom to access the course at any time they choose from any location (learn more at http://slisweb.sjsu.edu/prospective-students/discover-online-learning).

Example 2: Librarian-Taught Courses

At Penn State University, many librarians teach credit courses, and most do so within the library studies program. Opportunities for teaching in credit and noncredit courses and programs also occur through academic departments or university outreach and cooperative extension (learn more at http://www.libraries.psu.edu/psul/lls/toolkit.html).

Self-Paced Instruction

Instructional self-directed materials offer patrons access to the library 24 hours per day, 7 days per week, and take different formats:

- Subject research guides
- Course guides for use in classroom instruction or as stand-alone research portals
- Guides on how to use specific tools or technologies (e.g., EndNote, citation management)
- Instructional videos (e.g., how to use the library catalog)
- Individual on-demand videos to answer specific questions
- Online synchronous instruction
- Help pages on the library website
- Library information embedded in specific courses

Several examples illustrate how libraries are using self-paced instruction.

Example 1: Public Library Association's Self-Paced Courses

Turning the Page Online is a free library advocacy training course developed and presented by the Public Library Association. In this self-paced course, library staff and supporters learn how to create and tell their library's story, deliver effective presentations, develop a compelling case for support, and build and sustain partnerships along the way. Some of the eleven courses include

Making It Memorable (How to Sell Your Story and Get Results)

Staying on Track (Managing and Measuring Your Advocacy Project)

Show Me the Money (Tips for Making Public Funding Requests)

What's Next? (Preparing Your Advocacy Plan for Implementation)

Example 2: University of North Carolina Online Self-Paced Courses

The University of North Carolina offers different types of online courses for credit, depending on your student status. For example, distance education courses are offered on a semester schedule in the spring and fall and over an extended summer session. Students are not required to attend class, but they communicate with classmates and their instructor via e-mail and forums. Self-paced courses are online courses that can be completed at a student's own pace. Students can enroll at any time of year, and no class attendance is required.

⟲ Tap Other Sources of Training

With the ever-changing nature of their work, library staff need fresh and innovative training opportunities to stay current and continue to meet the needs of their patrons. A time-saving and often cost-effective way to provide intensive training is to outsource. There are different levels of outsourcing. For example, lessons, handouts, vendors, and experts are available to provide education that will save the librarian precious time and energy.

The first level of outsourcing involves borrowing plans or ideas. A great way to get ideas for library lessons is to participate in library organizations, such as the American Library Association, Special Libraries Association, or Public Library Association. Review their websites, join their blogs, register for their online e-newsletters or training sessions, or sign up for their social media (e.g., Facebook, Twitter). Patrons at different public libraries often have similar wants and needs, so librarians can tap state libraries or check the Internet for instructional materials. University libraries offer many materials in different content-related areas. Vendors of library materials—particularly databases, such as ProQuest and Dialog—often offer training and orientation to new users on their products, as well as updates to experienced users. Check their websites and social media for instruction they offer.

Professional associations, conferences, and continuing education programs are natural sources to build a community of practice. As the capacity to support rich communication experiences online continues to expand, many digital forums have been developed that provide librarians with the means to interact with like-minded colleagues. Professional organizations such as the Association of College and Research Libraries (for academic libraries) offer frequent digital learning opportunities, while smaller in-person events, such as m-Libraries, provide digital resources and components, all excellent for networking at no cost.

Through a combination of tools—such as webcasting, blogging, chat, and threaded discussion to create hybrid or all-online learning environments—networking sites and conferences often allow users to create personal profiles, access resources and programs, and interact with professionals who share similar interests. ALA Connect (http://connect.ala.org), the American Library Association's virtual collaborative workspace, provides a space for not only committee work but also web-based learning communities and interest groups on a range of topics. In addition, the community section of Educause (http://www.educause.edu/community) provides a technology-oriented discussion platform.

Community elements are inherent in many of the online spaces available to learners and instructors. Blogs, wikis, Twitter, LinkedIn, and Facebook all have potential as learning communities. Excellent group blogs that often deal with instruction include In the Library with the Lead Pipe (http://www.inthelibrarywiththeleadpipe.org), ACRLog (http://acrlog.org), and WebJunction (http://www.webjunction.org). Nonlibrary blogs, especially academic ones such as ProfHacker (http://chronicle.com/blogs/profhacker/), are useful for pedagogical and technological inspiration and tips about teaching, technology, and productivity.

Some libraries partner with local groups. The Chicago Public Library offers a variety of teaching venues for adults and children. The library brings in guest experts. A free legal information series focuses on hot legal issues, such as adoption and starting a small business. Financial experts discuss budgeting and financial planning.

Another program, Teachers in the Library, helps students use appropriate learning strategies, find the best resources for completing homework assignments, and answer questions for parents regarding their children's homework. CyberNavigators offer small group classes and one-on-one sessions for seniors on Internet basics.

⊚ Key Points

The diversity of instructional techniques, especially those emphasizing learner-centered activities, is the wave of the future (see table 4.1 for more resources). By modeling libraries using direct, learner-based, and self-paced instruction, whether face-to-face or online, instruction librarians can meet the needs of their patrons in public, academic, and special libraries. As such, chapter 5 focuses on face-to-face instruction, chapter 7 on online synchronous teaching, and chapter 8 on self-paced learning.

Table 4.1. URLs for Chapter 4

DESCRIPTION	URL
Events offered by the public library	http://www.chipublib.org/events
Public library instruction curriculum, courses, and lesson outline	http://digitalcommons.macalester.edu/cgi/viewcontent.cgi?article =1119&context=libtech_conf
Information about the embedded librarian	http://ist511embedded.wikispaces.com/file/view/ Background+on+Embed+Lib.pdf
Association of College and Research Libraries standards	http://www.ala.org/ala/acrl/acrlstandards/ informationliteracycompetency.cfm http://www.ala.org/acrl/standards/characteristics
Sample public library	http://digitalcommons.macalester.edu/cgi/viewcontent.cgi?article =1119&context=libtech_conf
Examples of schools offering self-paced courses	http://www.elearners.com/online-education-resources/ online-learning/self-paced-education/

EXERCISES: Now You Try It . . .

To reinforce what you learned in this chapter, try the following exercises:

1. You are working with another facilitator in your organization. The two of you get along well, and a friendship has started to form. Most times, you team-teach the workshops. You notice that sometimes the learners seem to get distracted when your partner (Simon) is teaching. You have also observed that he likes to talk for long periods, and when he does so, he often reads extensively from his notes. In groups of three,
   * Brainstorm at least three reasons why the learners may be distracted while Simon is teaching.

- Formulate suggestions for how Simon could improve his delivery.
- Anticipate how Simon may react to the feedback you want to give him. How will this influence how you give your constructive feedback?
- Follow the guidelines for giving constructive feedback: Write out what you will say and how you will say it. Remember that constructive feedback is a mix of positive (improving or strengthening) and negative comments.

2. Now role-play the feedback session. Ask one person to give feedback, one to receive it, and the other to observe.

3. After you have finished the role-play, discuss these questions within your group.

   Observer—How did you observe feedback being given and received? What was effective? What could be improved next time? Share these thoughts with your group.

   Giver—What was difficult in organizing and giving feedback? What worked well? What would you improve the next time?

   Receiver—What was difficult about receiving the feedback? Describe your response to it. What worked well? What would you like to improve for next time?

4. After exploring the modes of instruction and methods to deliver instruction, create a chart comparing different approaches.
   - Create a table with URLs for each method you select, with three columns: website name, URL, and description.
   - Select a topic and discuss how it might be approached in different ways using several techniques.

5. Determine the instruction that you want to incorporate in your library. Select a topic, and write a lesson plan. Try the lesson with patrons, and evaluate the results (see chapter 3 on lesson planning).

Reference

Merrill, M. D. 2002. "First Principles of Instruction." *Educational Technology Research and Development* 50 (3): 43–59.

Further Reading

Association of College and Research Libraries, American Library Association. 2003. "Characteristics of Programs of Information Literacy That Illustrate Best Practices: A Guideline." http://www.ala.org/ala/acrl/acrlstandards/characteristics.cfm.

———. 2006. "Information Literacy Competency Standards for Higher Education." http://www.ala.org/acrl/ilcomstan.html.

Clark, R. C., and R. E. Mayer. 2003. *E-Learning and the Science of Instruction*. San Francisco: Jossey-Bass Pfeiffer.

Instruction Section, Association of College and Research Libraries. 2008. "*The First-Year Experience and Academic Libraries: A Select, Annotated Bibliography*." http://www.ala.org/ala/mgrps/divs/acrl/about/sections/is/projpubs/tmcfyebib.cfm.

Kesselman, Martin A., and Sarah Barbara Watstein. 2009. "Creating Opportunities: Embedded Librarians." *Journal of Library Administration* 49 (4): 383–400.

Lietzau, Z., and J. Helgren. 2011. *U.S. Public Libraries and the Use of Web Technologies, 2010.* Denver, CO: Colorado State Library, Library Research Service. http://www.lrs.org/documents/web20/ WebTech2010_CloserLookReport_Final.pdf.

Marzano, R. J., D. J. Pickering, and J. E. Pollock. 2001. *Classroom Instruction That Works: Research-Based Strategies for Increasing Student Achievement.* Alexandria, VA: Association for Supervision and Curriculum Development.

Oakleaf, M. 2010. *The Value of Academic Libraries: A Comprehensive Research Review and Report.* Chicago: Association of College and Research Libraries.

Rosenshine, B. 1997. "Advances in Research on Instruction." In *Issues in Educating Students with Disabilities*, edited by E. J. Lloyd, E. J. Kameanui, and D. Chard, 197–221. Mahwah, NJ: Erlbaum.

CHAPTER 5

Face-to-Face Presentations

THE *Museums, Libraries, and 21st Century Skills* report, created by the Institute of Museum and Library Services (2009), describes ways that libraries can help their patrons enhance their skills through instruction:

- Offer programs and classes that explore new ideas and opportunities.
- Customize programs to heighten audience engagement; offer at times when target audiences can easily participate.
- Design programs and classes to include consideration of twenty-first-century skills as learning outcomes (interactive, focused on project-based learning, emphasis on teamwork, etc.).
- Ensure that programs provide twenty-first-century context for the unemployed in the current job market.
- Provide opportunities for patrons' peer-to-peer knowledge sharing and networking.
- Encourage the use of current technology tools for virtual connection through online communities and social networks.
- Seek to stimulate creative thinking and encourage innovation.

Chapter 4 outlines different types of instruction, modes of instruction, and delivery methods that incorporate some of these goals. This chapter focuses on one aspect of teaching—face-to-face instruction: workshops, embedded instruction librarians, small groups, and one-on-one training in academic settings, public libraries, and special libraries. Lesson plans provide models of instruction to help you create your own lessons. Topics chosen for the lessons are ones deemed most desirable to patrons.

⊚ Getting Ready for Face-to-Face Training: What Should You Consider?

When you are conducting a workshop or other face-to-face training, you need to consider factors such as your appearance, presentation materials, handouts, and strategies.

Your Presence Counts

Communicate your information as clearly and accurately as possible to your students or patrons. It is natural to feel stage fright when asked to present to a group, even a small one, especially if you do not do it often. Controlling all aspects of the training environment will help you know and understand your subject matter and practice what and how you plan to present it. Review the presentation in your mind, and make sure that everything you will use during the presentation is ready and organized. Leave nothing to chance.

One tip is to develop a pretraining checklist and check off everything that you will use—for example, a PowerPoint presentation, handouts, and technology needed. If you will be demonstrating online, make sure that you can connect to your library network. Important too is the layout—room arrangement and environment conditions. You want to project yourself as being a skilled professional with authoritative sources of knowledge that your students can learn from, and being well organized is just one more way of maintaining that image of a professional.

You get only one chance to make that first impression from the moment you appear before your class and start your speech or presentation. On average, you have between one and two minutes at most to set the tone of your session. Some say that you have even less time than that to capture the attention of attendees and begin to motivate them.

A couple of tips to consider: First, the image that you project with your attire lends a level of credibility. Your clothes and accessories provide a self-portrait of you. Your appearance can also help you handle some of the tough issues that pop up from time to time during your presentation as a teacher, trainer, or speaker. Second, interacting with your students by asking or answering questions can and does make for a dynamic training and learning environment, where everyone is learning directly or indirectly from your responses to the questions being asked. Remember—depending on what method of instruction you are conducting, managing and answering questions from your students is an integral part of your training setting:

- Always turn and face directly to the person asking the question. In some cases, you may need to repeat the question so that everyone in the audience can hear it and benefit from your answer.

- In a situation where you are not immediately able to respond to the person asking the question, do not ignore him or her. Make every effort possible to acknowledge that person and question, with either a hand signal or a nod that you heard the student.
- If you do not know the answer to the question being asked, just say so! The worst thing that you can do is to give a response that does not answer the question.

Keeping your audience motivated, listening, and interacting with you requires work on your part. Here are a few suggestions that may help:

- Change your voice pitch and speed.
- Use gestures (the art of using your hands).
- Tell a joke (be careful to keep it clean and mundane).
- Move away from a podium whenever possible.
- Interact with your audience, ask a question.

Concluding remarks count! As you begin to finish your presentation, your closing remarks must remain as strong as when you started. Remember—you want them to retain what you are telling them.

Make Visuals Work for You

There are many types of media available to make your visuals pleasing and to keep the way that people prefer to receive their information in mind at the same time. For example, a kinesthetic learner likes hands-on activities or audience participation; a visual learner leans toward a demonstration; and the auditory learner prefers an organized talk spoken in a clear, enthusiastic voice.

There are numerous opinions on how to develop your visual aids. Will you use PowerPoint slides (the most common option), podcasts, graphs and charts, pictures and photographs, flipcharts, or a whiteboard? Will you incorporate video, use technology to demonstrate online, and have attendees interact with the technology? These are just some of the possibilities to provide visual motivation to your students. Deciding on strategies is important because your visual aids can make or break your instruction, resulting in a complete failure of the overall effectiveness of your presentation. URLs to consult for more ideas can be found at the end of the chapter.

Handouts

Handouts are an important part of a workshop. It is a good idea to create them at the same time that you are planning your session. This ensures that the information you include will be tailored to that specific course. In general, handouts should include an outline of the key ideas in your presentation, to which students will want to refer later. Information for further research is useful, such as a bibliography, illustrations, charts, and graphics. A part of the handout might include an activity guide with directions.

The design of your handout counts. That does not mean that it should be fancy, and it should definitely not be wordy—the urge to say too much can ruin a good handout. Set off distinct parts of the handout, using italics, shading, bolding, or underlining. Use bullet lists to make them easier to scan and understand. Plenty of white space makes what is on the handout stand out, especially when using Serif fonts such as Times New Roman, which are distinct in print. Stick to no more than three fonts in a handout, and one handout per session avoids confusion.

When you have completed the handout, look at it and ask yourself the following questions:

- Does the information flow? Is it coordinated with your presentation?
- Is the handout visually appealing—readable, concise, noncluttered?
- Will the handout help the student recall main ideas?
- Is your contact information included?
- Are helpful websites or tips for finding additional information included?

For more on creating handouts, see chapter 3.

Instructional Strategies

How you plan to deliver your instruction is most effective when employed to meet particular learning goals and objectives. So start off by asking and answering this key question: What are the major learning goals and objectives for the instruction that you plan to create? Once these goals and objectives have been identified and clearly articulated, you can then address the question of which learning strategies, activities, and experiences to employ. Different strategies offer advantages and disadvantages for different audiences, learning styles, and goals that you have for your instruction.

Selecting a Topic for the Academic Workshop

An Educational Testing Service (2007) study of approximately 6,300 college and high school students in 63 schools found that students had insufficient ability to evaluate websites and social media sites:

- 52 percent judged the objectivity of the sites correctly;
- 65 percent judged the authority correctly;
- 72 percent judged the timeliness correctly; and
- 49 percent of test takers identified the one website that met all criteria.

Given the need for information in the twenty-first century, learners must know how to find it, how to focus it, and how to filter out nonsense. But for many students, their main source for information is Google. According to a study by the Pew Research Center, today's students determine relevancy of sources most often by common sense (80 percent), cross-checking (71 percent), reputation of source, and credible recommendations—hardly a scientific way of evaluating sources (Zickuhr, Rainie, and Purcell, 2013). Undergrad students use Wikipedia and Google most; graduate students seek advice from faculty, dissertation advisors, mentors, and electronic databases.

The academic librarian's role is to ensure that students, faculty, and staff are effective users of information. Information literacy forms the basis for lifelong learning. It is common to all disciplines, all learning environments, and all levels of education. It enables learners to master content and extend their investigations, become more self-directed, and assume greater control over their learning.

What Is Information Literacy?

An American Library Association report (1989) defines information literacy as follows:

> A person must be able to recognize when information is needed and have the ability to locate, evaluate, and use effectively the needed information. Information literate people are those who have learned how to learn. They know how to find information, and how to use information in such a way that others can learn from them. They are people prepared for lifelong learning because they can always find the information needed for any task or decision at hand.

Cornell University Libraries (http://olinuris.library.cornell.edu/content/instruction) describe one criterion of an information-literate student: an individual who can select and search appropriate databases to discover useful articles and evaluate information sources critically according to selected criteria (e.g., scholarly authority, currency, bias) to select pertinent sources. Librarians can teach patrons how to evaluate websites and social media sites in a variety of settings:

- librarian–student interactions at the reference desk;
- librarian–student interactions during telephone, e-mail, and question-and-answer reference interactions;
- faculty incorporating problem-based research assignments into the curriculum;
- faculty sharing disciplinary research expertise with students in the classroom; and
- librarians working with classes in library instruction sessions, often utilizing active learning projects and exercises developed through faculty–librarian collaboration.

Much research mentioned thus far indicates that students turn to the Internet for many sources of class assignments. This has advantages and disadvantages. The web is easy to use; it contains a wealth of information from a variety of sources worldwide on every subject imaginable. However, unlike library resources—where the books, journals, and other materials have already been evaluated by scholars, publishers, and librarians using standard criteria—there is no formal standardized evaluation for information on the Internet.

Documents on the web range in quality. Sites exist containing information from authors with excellent credentials and others whose only credentials are their desires to express their opinions. Because it is easy to publish a website or information on a social media site, visitors never know what material they will find there. It could be from reputable sources, such as universities, museums, educational organizations, and companies, or it could be from individuals whose opinions have little or no substantiation. Users of the Internet are none the wiser if they cannot differentiate among sites and evaluate the quality of the information on them.

As you plan your lesson, you must have at hand material that you can draw from on the topic that you plan to teach, in this case "evaluating web resources." The information that follows outlines information necessary to form your background and offer concrete material to your students.

Evaluation Criteria

If individuals—whether they are undergraduate or graduate students or patrons in the public library—are planning to conduct research, they must be able to spot bias, identify unwarranted claims, and determine whether an argument has sufficient factual support. Using the information for research is only part of the benefit. Skills performed to find information and assess its accuracy, currency, and reputation are also important life-learning tools that librarians and teachers want to instill in their students. These skills can be improved when they evaluate websites.

Five traditional criteria used to determine the quality of print information in libraries can also be applied to the evaluation of web resources. Many educational groups, including the American Library Association and universities, have created their own sets of criteria. The sample that follows has been categorized by combining criteria from many sources. Handout 5.1 can be presented as is or adapted to fit more closely to one's research needs and experience.

Authority

To determine the authorship of a website, examine the page closely for information about the author to see if anyone else has contributed to the site. Determining the source or sponsor of a website can be helpful in evaluating the usefulness of the information on each page. Websites can be sponsored by individuals who set up personal sites, corporations who want to advertise and sell products and services, government organizations (e.g., the Library of Congress), professional organizations (e.g., the Special Libraries Association), and educational institutions (e.g., universities and public libraries). Check information on webpages to see if it includes references. Social media sites—blogs, Twitter, Facebook, YouTube—may contain information from both sources: They may be opinions of individuals and videos created for fun, or they may be the work of authoritative sources (e.g., health tips from the American Medical Association).

There are other ways to check for information about authors:

- Search the links to information about the author, usually found at the bottom of a page.
- Check the headers and footers for the author's name, title, credentials, or affiliation.
- Look for telling extensions in the domain name: edu, org, gov, com, net.
- Look at any contact information, such as "About us" or "Contact us."
- Search the author's name on Google for other publications.
- Check to see if the author has created other websites with more information about him or her.
- Check to see if the author or contributor to a webpage has published in print. If so, do these print sources provide you with additional information on the author and what qualifications he or she might have?

Accuracy

To determine how reliable and free from error the information contained on a website is, remember to look at who is hosting the site. Is it a university, a government organization, a professional association, a commercial host, an advocacy group, a publisher? What are

HANDOUT 5.1. Criteria for Evaluating Websites

Website title: _____

URL: _____

Date: _____ Time: _____

Directions: Assign a point value to each section based on the following criteria (1 = *poor*, 5 = *excellent*).

Authority/Credibility = 20 points
_____ Objective, balanced presentation of material
_____ Expertise of individual or group who created site identified
_____ Bias-free viewpoints expressed
_____ Contact information for author/designer available on the site

Content = 20 points
_____ Accurate, reliable information
_____ Purpose of site clear
_____ Content detailed
_____ Content structured with headings to delineate sections

Accessibility = 20 points
_____ Site or locator map available
_____ External and internal links active
_____ Navigation icons consistent throughout site
_____ Site loads quickly

Currency = 15 points
_____ Regularity of site updates identified
_____ Includes a publication date or a "last updated" date on the site
_____ Includes a date of copyright

Design Features = 25 points
_____ Site well designed and consistent with uncluttered pages and useful subheadings
_____ Intuitive icons, menus, and directional symbols for ease of use
_____ Options for printing and/or downloading text and graphics available
_____ Text on site follows basic principles of grammar, spelling, and composition
_____ Graphics at the site serve purpose

its biases? A good website should state its purpose and intended audience. It is always a good idea to check with other web resources, journals, or magazines that publish website reviews to see if the site has received a stamp of approval and, if so, by whom. Always remember to verify the information on the website with information found in other print- and web-based sources.

To verify the credibility of the information, find out about the author, especially if that person is unknown to you. Ask yourself these questions: Is the author an expert or qualified to present the information? Does the page that you are viewing link back to the homepage of a well-known organization? Is the page signed—name and credentials? Is it an official site of a credible agency (e.g., CNN) or some individual's homepage?

Objectivity

To determine the objectivity of a website, check if advertising and informational content are being supplied by the same person or organization. If so, examine whether there is a bias to the informational content. Keep in mind that many websites with excellent information are sponsored by commercial entities or take advertisements to finance the site.

Ask the following questions when trying to determine how objective material on a site is:

- Do the sponsors of the site have a vested interest in the viewpoint presented?
- Are links to other viewpoints balanced—unbiased?
- Do the authors use persuasive techniques to try to sway opinion?
- Are affiliations clear?
- Does advertising appear on the page?
- Could graphics for affiliations potentially bias the information presented?
- Can the potential audience for the site be determined?

Currency

A website's currency can be important, especially if you are looking for statistics. To determine the currency of a website, check when the page was created and last updated. Also look to see if there are broken links on the site; it could be an indication of an abandoned page. Check also to see how often new links and new material appear on the site.

Coverage

To determine if the information is adequately covered on a website, compare the information with that found on other websites. Does one site provide more information, more references, more contacts? Also compare the information on the website with that available in print sources, such as books, journals, and reports, if available.

The 2.5-hour workshop/class that follows provides a model that can be offered by an embedded librarian in an academic setting. It focuses on the basic concepts for evaluating web resources. The lesson plan describes and illustrates how to go about teaching students to evaluate online information sources. This is just one aspect of information literacy, but it is vital to individuals working in the twenty-first century.

⊚ Lesson Plan Model on Evaluating Web Sources

The following step-by-step procedures provide the "how-to" to teach participants how to think critically when evaluating sources of information that they plan to use in research. The lesson describes and illustrates models of appropriate resources based on the evaluation criteria discussed earlier in this chapter. Practice sessions reinforce the learning and handouts from the instruction.

Step 1: Conduct a Needs Assessment

The analysis phase is the building block of a training program. The basis for who must be trained, what must be learned, when training will occur, and where the training will take place are accomplished in this phase. The product of this phase is the foundation for all subsequent development activities. During this phase, it is also important to look at how you are going to evaluate the learning that you want to take place. A needs assessment of participants should be completed in advance, with requirements for participating in the instruction. For example, attendees at this workshop should be familiar with computer basics, including logging onto and using a web browser.

Step 2: Write the Lesson Goal and Objectives

Employ backward design to make the workshop content relevant. Start by figuring out the learning outcomes you want students or patrons to achieve. Design goals and objectives so they are attainable. They should be stated in terms of learner behavior and built around change in the learner. They could be skills or processes attendees will master or a list of tasks they will be able to perform at the end of the workshop. These goals and objectives help you decide on your teaching methods and evaluation practices.

Writing goals and objectives for any lesson is important to keep you on track and for you and your students to know where you are heading and how you will get there.

Lesson Goal

The goal for this lesson is for students to

- Build skills to differentiate web resources and social media sites based on specific criteria

Lesson Objectives

At the end of the workshop, attendees should be able to

- Use evaluation criteria to assess web resources
- Determine the purpose of a website
- Identify advantages and disadvantages of social media resources, including Twitter, blogs, and Facebook
- Compare and contrast websites and social media
- Access and evaluate at least five web resources appropriate for their research

Step 3: Create the Instruction

A workshop or class should have a beginning, middle, and end. When creating the instruction, you will introduce the lesson, provide activities and interaction, and follow up for retention.

Introduce the Workshop: Ten Minutes

If you are at this point in the chapter, you already read what you should think about in advance of the actual workshop (in preplanning)—that is, general details to remember at the outset of a workshop. Let's get started with the lesson. Once you have completed those tasks, do the following

1. Indicate that participants will be working together as they learn about evaluating web resources.
2. Explain that you will not discuss everything there is to know about evaluating websites but that students will be able systematically, using specific criteria, to determine the worth of a site by the end of the workshop.
3. Ask attendees to introduce themselves, including how much time they have spent on the Internet looking at different websites. This will help you determine ability levels as you assign groups for the warm-up exercise.
4. Review the agenda for the workshop, describing what you will cover, the time frame for each activity, and why it is important. Indicate that students will be actively participating in group work to complete practice exercises.
5. Review the objectives for the workshop with participants.

Begin the Warm-Up Exercise: Twenty Minutes

Begin the warm-up exercise. Completing this task should help you assess how critically participants are able to view web resources.

1. Assign groups of three based on the information that you obtained about their familiarity with web sources during the introductions. You may want to combine participants who are familiar with web searching with those who have not had much experience. They can then help each other.
2. Hand out instructions for the exercise, with a website included, and tell attendees that they should follow the directions and evaluate the site in their groups. Indicate that each team will then have a few minutes to explain its assessment of the site to the whole group. Sample websites are included in table 5.1.
3. Ask attendees to jot down notes to rely on when they present their evaluations. Have them list the reasons that they used in their evaluations on a large piece of paper. This activity is designed to start participants thinking immediately about the idea of evaluation when they are on the Internet. It will act as a pretest to the evaluation work that follows. Participants may know intuitively that they liked or disliked a particular site, but they may not be able to articulate why this was. By the end of the workshop, they should be able to identify and use specific criteria on which to base their judgments of web resources.

4. Mention that assessing web resources is much like evaluating printed resources. It takes practice and skill for them to be able to move beyond the enjoyment that they get from "surfing the web" to looking critically at the material that they find there.

5. Write down on a whiteboard the different criteria that groups used to evaluate their particular sites.

Table 5.1. Resources for Web Evaluation

DESCRIPTION	URL
Videos on evaluating websites	http://www.slideshare.net/angelasiefer/criteria-for-evaluating-webpages
Video with exercise on evaluation	http://www.slideshare.net/lenva/information-literacy-finding-information-presentation
Video with explanation of five criteria	http://www.slideshare.net/hisled/evaluating-information-sources-8820407
Good example for objectivity criteria	http://www.fairus.org/home
Good example for bias	http://www.mcclearyscientific.com
Questions to ask for evaluation of web sources	http://www.slideshare.net/hisled/evaluating-your-sources-4939461

Conduct Part 1: Evaluation Criteria—Fifteen Minutes

In part 1, you will instruct attendees on the importance of evaluating web resources for their research.

1. From the evaluation sheets, identify common criteria that groups came up with. Ask them why they felt that a specific point was important.

2. Explain the benefit of building critical thinking for lifelong learning as an added benefit to finding appropriate material on the Internet. (Use figure 2.3, if appropriate, for your attendees.) Mention that information literacy skills require higher levels of critical thinking.

3. Distribute handout 5.1 and review any criteria not included on their warm-up sheets. Ask why certain criteria should be included.

4. Choose one of these two potential ways to present the criteria:
   a. Use a straightforward listing of criteria, with characteristics and questions to ask for each.
   b. Use an inductive approach to teach understanding of the criteria. Write the first category on the whiteboard. Ask attendees to identify what is important to them about websites that relates to this criterion (e.g., site creators and what credentials they have related to the information presented at the site—as in a doctor discussing causes of arthritis). Refer back to their experiences during the warm-up exercise as a reference point. List the criteria they mention under Category 1—Authority. Continue in the same way with the remaining categories. Add points that the students do not mention under each category.

Conduct Part 2: Website Evaluation—15 Minutes

You will model the steps to evaluate the Journal of the American Medical Association's website using the criteria you reviewed in part 1 (see table 5.1 for more on website evaluation).

1. From your web browser, log on to the site by typing http://jama.jamanetwork.com/issue.aspx.
2. Look at the home page that appears. Use the criteria just reviewed as a basis for analyzing it.
3. Point out the amount of text and the topics provided. Note the reading level, the lack of pictures. Point out the diversity, the colorful graphics, and limited amount of text. Ask attendees who they think the audience is for this site and to give characteristics of the group.
4. Check subsequent pages of the website to determine that content is appropriate—nonbiased, current, and easily accessible. Distribute handout 5.2. Tell attendees they can use it in a minilesson to teach "detecting bias" before they have their students view websites.
5. Allow for a twenty-minute online practice so that participants can reevaluate the websites they looked at in the warm-up exercise, only this time using specific criteria. Have them use handout 5.1. *Note:* For librarians working with children in a public library, use handout 5.3 (a more simplistic evaluation sheet).
6. Following the online practice, conduct a debriefing session (ten minutes) by asking attendees to reflect on the web evaluations they completed. You can have them do this orally or by writing comments in their notebooks.
7. Following the debriefing, have students take a ten-minute break.

Conduct Part 3: Social Media Evaluation—Forty-Five Minutes

Social media sites are legitimate communication tools and can be a fast way to get all kinds of information from people whom you already know as well as the rest of the world. For example, in cases of disasters, flu outbreaks, or other emergencies where timeliness is key, social media has proved quite useful. But there is no quick way to evaluate the information that you find on social networking sites. Anyone can register any identity on any social networking site. Make sure to pay close attention to where the information comes from and to back up what you see with information from authoritative sources.

To become effective and comfortable with social media sites, have attendees explore some blogs, Twitter, and Facebook sites.

1. Ask participants if they have used social media such as Facebook, Twitter, or blogs. Have them indicate their purposes for using them and to name some.
2. In groups of three, have attendees brainstorm (five minutes) reasons why they might want to use social media for their research projects. List all results on one common sheet.
3. Identify authoritative uses for social media and how the sites meet evaluation criteria. For those who have used these sources for research, ask them to write down the URLs for others to view.

HANDOUT 5.2. Detecting Bias

Bias is a subtle attempt to influence opinion, to express a preference or prejudice. Bias can be an opinion disguised as fact. The following are examples of ways that bias can appear in the news:

Bias through selection and omission: Editors who choose to use or not use a specific news item can express bias by, for example, catering to young readers because they spend more money and ignoring news of interest to the elderly. Details within a story are ignored while others are included that give readers a different opinion of the events reported. For example, if a few people boo during a speech, this display can be described as "remarks greeted by jeers" or the reaction can be ignored as "a handful of dissidents." This type of bias is difficult to detect without comparing and contrasting the same event as reported in different papers.

Bias through placement: Front-page stories are often judged by readers as more significant than those residing on inside pages. Television and radio newscasts run the important stories first. For instance, by giving prominent space to all shootings and gun-related accidents in the paper, an editor can campaign against owning handguns.

Bias by headline: Headlines are the most-read part of a paper, and many people scan nearly all headlines, which can convey excitement where little exists, express approval or condemnation, and steer public opinion.

Bias by photos, captions, and camera angles: Pictures can flatter a person or make him or her look unpleasant. For example, during an election campaign, a paper can choose photos to influence opinion about a candidate.

Bias through use of names and titles: Labels and titles that describe people, places, and events can reflect bias and influence opinion. For instance, the same person can be called a "terrorist," a "leader of the people's army," or a "freedom fighter."

Bias through statistics and crowd counts: To make a disaster seem more spectacular and thus more worthy of reading, numbers can be inflated. "Two hundred injured in soccer match" can be the same as "only minor injuries at the soccer match." Crowd counts are often inaccurate and reflect the opinion of the person doing the counting.

Bias through source control: Consider where the news item comes from, such as a reporter, an eyewitness, police officer or firefighter, or elected or appointed government official. Some stories are supplied by companies or public relations directors to advocate support for their products or services.

Bias through word choice and tone: The words chosen, just as in headlines, can influence the opinion of the news reader.

HANDOUT 5.3. Criteria for Children to Evaluate Websites

Website title: _____

URL: _____

Date: _____ Time: _____ Grade level: _____

Directions: Assign a point value to each section based on the following criteria (1 = *poor*, 5 = *excellent*).

Design

1 2 3 4 5   Easily move from page to page

1 2 3 4 5   Good use of color

1 2 3 4 5   Graphics necessary

Content

1 2 3 4 5   Information is useful

1 2 3 4 5   Additional resource links included

1 2 3 4 5   How site content compares to similar sites

Technical Parts

1 2 3 4 5   All links work

1 2 3 4 5   Site appears quickly

Authority

1 2 3 4 5   Name of host is stated

1 2 3 4 5   Contact person is named with e-mail address

1 2 3 4 5   Last update of site is given

4. Review three social media sites, and ask attendees how they would evaluate them (fifteen minutes). Use this medical Twitter site, #melanoma at https://twitter.com/search?q=%23melanoma&src=hash; the CNN money blog, at http://money.cnn.com; and a holistic medical blog, at http://breslowmed.tumblr.com.

5. Begin a twenty-minute online practice to reinforce the section on social media. Distribute handout 5.4.

6. In groups of three, have students use a class assignment that they need to research. Have them identify at least two social media sites on the topic that they might use and at least one that they would not consider. *Note:* For those who are not familiar with social media sites, they can select from the ones listed:
   • http://jama.jamanetwork.com/journal.aspx
   • http://blogs.library.jhu.edu/wordpress/
   • http://zapatopi.net/treeoctopus/
   • http://www.librariesthriving.org/workshops/upcomingseminars

7. Debrief the session (five minutes) by having groups comment on the exercises—what went well? what did they find that they did not expect? how useful were the sites they visited? were sites appropriate for a research topic?

Provide Follow-Up: The Next Step—Five Minutes

Follow-up for the workshop must provide attendees with more opportunities to evaluate web resources. It will keep the skills and concepts learned in this workshop fresh in their minds. Use handout 5.1.

1. Tell participants that they should continue to gather and review web resources for their next research project in any class during the next two weeks and annotate information about the sites in their notebooks.

2. Remind them of the value of evaluation in improving their critical thinking skills. Emphasize that evaluation is at the high end of Bloom's taxonomy.

Step 4: Evaluate Performance—Fifteen Minutes

You will be evaluating attendees' performance and understanding throughout the workshop. As part of this workshop evaluation, try the following:

1. Monitor students as they work on the Internet in the two practice sessions. Note the processes that they use to answer the questions in the exercises, and make suggestions as they work.

2. Review the web evaluation sheets that they completed during online practice sessions to see how effectively they can identify the strengths and weaknesses of web resources.

3. Have participants send you e-mail describing the sites that they will visit in the next two weeks that they think are most useful for their next research project. You might even compile a list to distribute to attendees of the best sites reviewed during the workshop.

4. Distribute handout 5.5. Ask participants to fill out the Self-Evaluation Checklist to see how well they accomplished the objectives of the workshop.

5. Distribute handout 5.6. This overall workshop evaluation form allows you to obtain feedback from attendees on the content and presentation of the workshop.

HANDOUT 5.4. Criteria for Evaluating Social Media Sites

Directions: Check those items that apply from the following criteria, to evaluate the social media sites that you join and the types that you suggest to your patrons and students.

Networking Features
- ☐ Post a profile
- ☐ Update pictures
- ☐ Use instant messaging
- ☐ Tag photos and notifications
- ☐ Join and create groups based on interests
- ☐ Share music playlists and videos

Profile
- ☐ Create a profile easily
- ☐ Reflect your personality, thoughts, and feelings
- ☐ Post photographs
- ☐ Interact with network of friends

Search
- ☐ Find friends and expand relationships
- ☐ Search for other members in safe, easy-to-use environment
- ☐ Search by name, city, school, and e-mail address

Security
- ☐ Provide privacy customization
- ☐ Set profile or parts of it to public or private
- ☐ Report inappropriate behavior and content
- ☐ Block specific people entirely

Accuracy
- ☐ Has the site existed for a while?
- ☐ Who did the person first "follow" or "friend"?
- ☐ Who first followed them?
- ☐ Who has spoken to them online?
- ☐ Who has spoken about them?
- ☐ Can you correlate this account with others?

HANDOUT 5.5. Self-Evaluation Checklist

Name: _____

Workshop title: _____

Directions: You have successfully completed this workshop when you are able to check each item in the lists below.

Evaluating Websites
☐ Name at least four criteria to use in evaluating a website.
☐ List three reasons to evaluate a site.
☐ Evaluate a website based on at least three criteria.
☐ Name three ways to determine that a website has credibility.
☐ List three design principles that a website should follow.
☐ Ask four questions to judge the quality of content on a site.
☐ Identify at least five good websites, and explain why they are worth using.

Evaluating Social Media
☐ Identify at least one social networking site that fits your personality and explain why.
☐ Create a social media profile.
☐ Name at least four criteria for evaluating social networking sites.
☐ Make a list of items you want to share on a social networking site.

HANDOUT 5.6. Participant Workshop Evaluation Example

1. What is your overall assessment of the workshop (1 = *insufficient*, 5 = *excellent*)?

   1   2   3   4   5

2. Which topics or aspects of the workshop did you find most interesting or useful?

   a. _____

   b. _____

   c. _____

   d. _____

3. Did the workshop achieve the agenda objectives?   Yes   No

   If no, why?

   _____

   _____

4. Knowledge and information gained from participation at this workshop?

   Met your expectations: Yes   No   Somewhat

   Will be useful/applicable in my work: Definitely   Mostly   Somewhat   Not at all

5. How do you think the workshop could have been made more effective?

   _____

   _____

6. Please comment on the organization of the workshop (1 = *insufficient*, 5 = *excellent*).

   1   2   3   4   5

7. Comments and suggestions (including activities or initiatives you think would be useful for the future)

   _____

   _____

8. Further comments or suggestions

   _____

   _____

Step 5: Summary and Wrap-Up—Five Minutes

1. Summarize the importance of evaluating web resources. Emphasize that evaluation is a technique that will help them build lifelong learning, as well as help them in their research projects.
2. Complete handout 5.7, which will allow you to assess how well you planned the workshop's content and tasks.

⑥ Lesson Plan Model: Small Group Instruction in the Public Library

Librarians are natural teachers. In the process of helping library users formulate research strategies, identify information sources, and discuss methods of accessing resources, librarians educate those they assist. Like most good teachers, the librarian's goal is to show library users how to become as self-sufficient as possible to ensure that intellectual pursuit and creativity are not frustrated.

The following lesson is designed for a small group in a public library but could be conducted as a workshop in any library. It provides active learning on social networking—specifically blogs, a popular form of social media. The lesson can be completed in one ninety-minute session or two forty-five-minute sessions.

Session 1: Learning about Blogs

In session 1, attendees learn what blogs are and how to access them, and they practice finding and reviewing them.

Step 1: Lesson Prep Work—Thirty Minutes before Workshop

Prepare the blogs you will be modeling to your group:

- Create account or log in to Blogspot, Tumblr, and Wordpress.
- Create posts and comments for each blog. See a model of a blog in figure 5.1 (on page 88).

Step 2: Write Lesson Goal and Objectives

This class is both for patrons who do not know what blogs are and have a curiosity about them and for those who would like to begin blogging themselves.

Lesson goal: Learners will review the mechanics of blogging, questioning, and commenting on blogs.

Lesson objectives: The learner will be able to accomplish the following tasks at the end of the lesson:

- Define "blog" and explain the popularity and uses of blogs in the modern world
- Find and read blogs
- Describe characteristics of several blogging platforms
- Create and maintain blogs of their own

HANDOUT 5.7. Workshop Instructor Assessment

Directions: Use this form to assess how well you think that you covered the main parts of the lesson. Take notes on the form so that you can return to your plan and make changes before using it again.

Objectives
Are objectives stated in terms of
- ☐ What the participants should learn?
- ☐ What they should be able to do, as evidence that they have learned?
- ☐ The time allotted for them—that is, adequate for learning and performing each objective?

Instruction
Does the plan cover what you are going to teach and how you will teach it?
- ☐ Yes
- ☐ No

What techniques have you planned to motivate students' interest—that is, the warm-up or "icebreaker"?
- ☐ Example
- ☐ Online work
- ☐ Question
- ☐ Visual demonstration
- ☐ Video
- ☐ Description of problem areas
- ☐ Other: _____

Have you provided an agenda to alert participants to what you will cover and what they will be expected to learn and do?
- ☐ Yes
- ☐ No

Is instruction organized so that each subtopic is introduced, taught, and reinforced with attendees before going to the next subtopic?
- ☐ Yes
- ☐ No

For each subtopic do you have some example or experience that attendees are likely to identify with?

☐ Yes

☐ No

Has instruction been sequenced cumulatively—that is, by giving "easier to learn" or "first necessary" material before harder, more complex material? Or, is the organization in a logical order?

☐ Cumulative

☐ Logical

Have you planned activities to follow up and reinforce what has been learned during the session?

☐ Yes

☐ No

Have you included means to evaluate the workshop in terms of the following?

☐ Content

☐ Activities

☐ Presentation

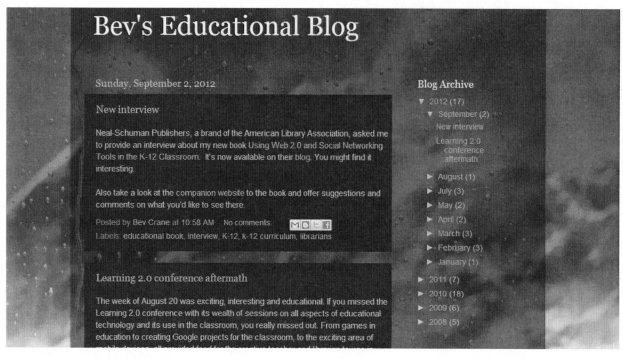

Figure 5.1. Blogspot blog sample.

Step 3: Introduce the Lesson—Ten Minutes

Begin with introductions and point out the logistics of the location. Review objectives so that patrons know what they will accomplish during the session.

Discussion: Write these questions on the whiteboard—"Do you read blogs, and if so, which ones?" "What do you want to learn today, specifically?"

Instructor introduction: Give blogging background, show personal blogs, and explain why you like to use blogs.

Step 4: Create the Instruction—Twenty Minutes

1. Explain what a blog is:
   - Show video about blogs at http://commoncraft.com/blog.
   - Define *web* + *log*, and give characteristics of a blog's informal writing style—often opinion, updated frequently, continuous stream, short, contains links.
   - Define a link—a connection from one website to another, usually indicated by a change in font (color and underlining), although a hyperlink can also be in a picture or video; your mouse becomes a hand when hovering over a link.
2. Show examples of blogs, and discuss what you would write about on your blog.

   Personal blogs—show your blog or that of someone you know or have researched. You can also select from the following blogs:

   > http://hcchrisp.blogspot.com
   > http://vitalitymentality.com
   > http//4in629.blogspot.com

http://www.whatimade.com
http://www.clouds365.com

Organizational blogs—if your library has a blog, show it, or use this one, http://blogs.westword.com (local). Also show shared blogs written by more than one person.

Business blogs—review this blog, http://findout.rei.com/blogs.

3. Activity 1: Locate Blogs—Twenty Minutes
   - Do a demonstration Google search for "best blogs" or "most-read blogs" or a more specific search, such as "NFL blog" or "fashion blog."
   - Have attendees click around to find blogs they like, and have them write down the URLs.
   - Have participants share with the group at least one blog that they liked.

Session 2: Working with Blogs—Fifty Minutes

Continuing with the same goal and objectives, restate the objectives from session 1 and explain what the group will be completing in this session. *Note:* If this is a separate second session, review briefly what you covered in session 1.

1. Explain what blogging platforms are, and identify three major ones: http://wordpress.com, http://www.tumblr.com, and http://www.blogspot.com.
2. Identify different parts of the blogs: navigation, tabs, about, posts, comments, linking. Ask patrons what features they like or dislike.

   Activity 1—Fifteen minutes: Divide group into pairs or triads. Have each small group review one blog and identify the parts just mentioned. Have each group teach the others about the blog it worked on by identifying the parts.

   Activity 2—Twenty minutes: Go through tabs: edit and publish posts. Have each small group select a blog other than the one it reviewed and make one or more posts, then move to a different blog and write comments to the posts.

3. If time, demonstrate how to change the design of a blog.

Step 5: Follow-Up—Five Minutes

1. Review hints for successful blogging.
   - Write about something that interests you—other people will find it interesting, too!
   - Learn from others—read other blogs, see what you like and do not like, and build those lessons into your blog.
   - Plan ahead—try to map out your first ten posts before you ever put something online. It will help you find your voice and refine what your blog is about.
   - Create a conversation—comment on other people's blogs (especially those that are writing about the same things you are) and they will return the favor.
   - Be consistent—the world will not end if you do not post something every day, but posting on a regular basis will build readers and subscribers. Set your own deadlines to put up content, and keep to it!
   - Expect writer's block and pace yourself—it is common to hit roadblocks or not feel inspired. Do not get discouraged, and plan ahead. Many blogging platforms let you

write posts in advance and schedule when they are to be posted, so you can keep posts coming while you take some time to get inspired again.

2. Remind patrons to practice—assign take-home exercises: write at least five comments on others' blogs during the week and create a blog and write at least three posts. Remind them that they can ask for help.

3. Ask patrons for feedback about new skills they learned or new connections they made. Ask them to think about how these skills may help them in their jobs, or ask what the next step is that they want to take in their learning about blogs.

Step 6: Evaluate the Results—Five Minutes

Evaluation for this lesson should be based on how well attendees interacted with members of the group and whether they were able to navigate at least one of the blogs demonstrated.

1. Have patrons complete the survey using handout 5.8.
2. Go over handout, review material, and emphasize further resources.

◎ Key Points

The teaching–learning process is dynamic and interactive (see table 5.2 for additional resources). As you begin face-to-face instruction in groups or with individuals, remember that each person participating in a workshop has responsibility for its success and failure. Significant learning takes place in a supportive climate that fosters interpersonal relationships between learners and the instructor. The content you present, the way you deliver it, and the reinforcements (including practice and handouts) will ensure that attendees leave your training session confident that they learned what you had planned in your objectives.

Table 5.2. URLs for Chapter 5

DESCRIPTION	URL
Ways to eliminate no-shows at training	http://www.techsoupforlibraries.org blog/a-commitment-to-patron-training
Manuals for teaching	http://www.kcls.org/instruction/manuals/
Sample topics for public training on technology	http://technologytrainingwheels.pbworks.com/w/page/20297631/ Teaching%20Technology
Staff and public library technology training	http://www.techsoupforlibraries.org/blog/ staff-and-public-technology-training-programs
Library use in the digital age survey	http://libraries.pewinternet.org/2013/01/22/Library-services/?utm_ source=Mailing+List&utm_campaign=66c42fe4cd-Library_ Services_01_22_2013&utm_medium=email
Articles on topics of interest to librarians	http://www.ala.org/lirt/sites/ala.org.lirt/files/content/jun12.pdf
Social media Tumblr sites	http://cheesepeople.tumblr.com http://thingsorganizedneatly.tumblr.com http://unamazing.com http://thisisinthappiness.com

HANDOUT 5.8. Group Participation Rubric

Directions: Reflect on the work you did as a group. Assess whether you worked well with your teammates, contributed to the team effort, and shouldered work equally. Answer the following questions:

1. Did you work hard, enjoy the project, and feel good about what you completed?
    _____
    _____

2. How much did you contribute to the group's project?
    _____
    _____

3. Could you keep up with the group? Did you finish your tasks on time?
    _____
    _____

4. If you had to do it again, would you do anything differently?
    _____
    _____

5. Did you assume any specific role within the group (e.g., leader, spokesperson, note taker)?
    _____
    _____

6. How would you say that you interact with your teammates?
    ☐ Listen and ask questions, offer ideas, never argue
    ☐ Listen but sometimes talk too much, rarely argue
    ☐ Usually do most of the talking, rarely allowing others to speak
    Comments: _____
    _____

7. How did you work with the group to organize, plan, and create a product?
    ☐ Effectively worked well
    ☐ Sometimes worked well
    ☐ Did not work well
    Comments: _____
    _____

The following exercises reinforce what you learned in this chapter and give you practice in setting up face-to-face instruction for your patrons.

1. Select at least five to ten websites on a subject (e.g., technology, English literature, business) for a workshop or class that you may be teaching in the library, for a faculty member's class, or as an embedded librarian.
   a. Using the five evaluation criteria, identify whether each website meets the criteria and what makes it appropriate or not for use in a research project.
   b. Select one appropriate site and one inappropriate site to use as models for your students.
   c. Based on the handouts in this chapter, create your own evaluation sheet for students.
   d. Create an assignment sheet based on the class subject area for a practice session during the workshop or as an outside assignment. Based on their level, give students websites to evaluate or ask them to select their own.
2. Locate several blogs of interest, review them at least three times a week, and write at least one comment to post on the blogs.
3. Choose a subject area, and do some research to locate five social media sites of different types (e.g., Twitter, Facebook, blogs) appropriate to the subject.
   a. Select one as an appropriate model based on the criteria discussed in this chapter.
   b. Set up a blog and create at least five posts on it. Try to add a post at least once a week so that bloggers will continue to come to your site.
4. Create an assignment for your students similar to the one cited for websites.
   a. Plan your instruction step-by-step: create an outline, write objectives, determine activities, and plan evaluation.
   b. As follow-up, provide a handout with evaluation criteria for students to use.

References

American Library Association. 1989. *American Library Association Presidential Committee on Information Literacy: Final Report.* Chicago: American Library Association. http://www.ala .org/acrl/publications/whitepapers/progressreport.

Educational Testing Service. 2007. "ETS: Educational Testing Service." http://www.ets.org.

Institute of Museum and Library Services. 2009. *Museums, Libraries, and 21st Century Skills* (IMLS-2009-NAI-01). Washington, DC: Institute of Museum and Library Services.

Zickuhr, Kathryn, Lee Rainie, and Kristen Purcell. 2013. "Library Services in the Digital Age." Pew Research Center. http://libraries.pewinternet.org/2013/01/22/library-services/.

Further Reading

Anderson, L. W., and David R. Krathwohl, eds. 2001. *A Taxonomy for Learning, Teaching, and Assessing: A Revision of Bloom's Taxonomy of Educational Objectives.* Boston: Allyn & Bacon.

Gerding, Stephanie. 2011. "Beyond Lecture: Training Delivery Methods." TechSoup for Libraries, March 23. http://bit.ly/MibgBP.

Kirkwood, Hal, and Kelly Evans. 2012. "Embedded Librarianship and Virtual Environments in Entrepreneurship Information Literacy: A Case Study." *Journal of Business and Finance Librarianship* 17 (1): 106–16.

Kuhlthau, C. C. 1994. *Teaching the Library Research Process.* 2nd ed. Metuchen, NJ: Scarecrow Press.

Li, Judy. 2012. "Serving as an Educator: A Southern Case in Embedded Librarianship." *Journal of Business and Finance Librarianship* 17 (2): 133–52.

"Partnership for 21st Century Skills." 2007. http://www.p21.org/storage/documents/21st_century_skills_assessment.pdf.

Seely, Sara Robertson, Sara Winstead Fry, and Margie Ruppel. 2011. "Information Literacy Follow-Through: Enhancing Preservice Teachers' Information Evaluation Skills through Formative Assessment." *Behavioral and Social Sciences Librarian* 30 (2): 72–84.

CHAPTER 6

Online Instruction

OBJECTIVES

After completing this chapter, you will be able to

▷ Define e-learning

▷ Explain the benefits and challenges of online instruction

▷ Discuss the differences between synchronous and asynchronous e-learning

▷ List traits that online learners should have

▷ Describe types of virtual training

▷ Describe planning involved in designing and delivering self-directed instruction

▷ Examine self-paced learning and its advantages

THE TWENTY-FIRST-CENTURY skills report by the Institute of Museum and Library Services (2009) identified ways that libraries can help their patrons enhance their skills. A goal is to connect patrons with online self-directed learning to

- identify learning opportunities that enhance twenty-first-century skills, such as critical thinking, problem solving, and collaboration;
- educate information seekers about the value of self-directed and online learning; and
- provide support for learners to develop skills and attitudes for success with self-directed learning.

Instruction in a library takes many forms. It occurs when a public library offers homework tutoring or when an academic library partners with another campus organization to provide a workshop in the student union. It happens when teacher librarians provide information literacy instruction for graduate students. Instruction librarians must assess the research and information evaluation skills of students, the unique needs of students at any level, and what teaching methods are appropriate to reach patrons with different requirements.

With the continued upsurge in new technologies, instruction librarians face a number of challenges, including staying abreast of the next new trend while continuing to engage users of all levels. As learners and classrooms evolve, what are the technology challenges that instruction librarians now face, and how do they stay afloat? This chapter addresses some of those issues.

This chapter discusses important issues surrounding live e-learning—its importance, who should take it, and more. It looks at synchronous and asynchronous learning and some of the advantages and disadvantages of each. Finally, examples illustrate libraries that are conducting online training and incorporating self-paced learning.

What Is E-Learning?

E-learning means "electronic learning"—it refers to a range of applications and processes designed to deliver instruction through electronic means. The definition of e-learning is broader than, but includes, "online learning" and "web-based training." It can be used to provide information and build specific job-related skills. Clark and Mayer define (2011) e-learning as

> instruction delivered on a computer via an Internet or intranet that includes content relative to the learning objective, using instructional methods such as examples and practice, along with media elements such as words and pictures to deliver the content and methods and build new knowledge and skills linked to individual learning goals or to improved performance.

Their focus is on e-learning to support individual learning and organizational goals—most often, the goal of special libraries.

Teaching online is not the same as teaching in person. For online teaching to be successful, instructors must do all course planning and development before the course begins. It is sometimes difficult to accommodate learning styles with online teaching, thereby making it necessary for instructors to go the extra mile for students struggling with the format of the class. It is also imperative that instructors keep up with communication with the students and provide rapid feedback.

Forms of E-Learning

E-learning can take different forms, some of which are illustrated in chapters 7 and 8:

Use of technology to enrich classroom and workplace learning: Internet, interactive multimedia, games/simulations, social networks

Online instruction such as webinars for distance learning: no face-to-face meetings

Blended instruction: combining online and face-to-face learning events

Synchronous: real time, multiple students online, instructor led

Asynchronous: students and instructor in intermittent interaction

Instructor-led group work: combining synchronous and asynchronous events

Self-study: online tutorials, research and discovery learning events

Self-study with subject matter expert: tutoring, mentoring, coaching

Web-based tutorials: individual or group using self-paced online resources

Video and audio resources: distributed by online streaming, download, or podcast

Every year the number of distance learning students grows, increasing the number that may never walk into brick-and-mortar libraries. Since the library's goal is to serve its patrons, it is often necessary to bring library services and instruction to them. Important capabilities of e-learning include the following:

Multimedia instruction: "anytime, anywhere," no instructor—asynchronous learning

Live "virtual classrooms," or webinars: synchronous learning

Streaming video and audio: with new broadband capabilities enhancing the next phase of rich media delivery

Internet phone: with VOIP (voice-over Internet protocol) telephony transforming the level of interactivity in virtual classrooms and allowing collaborative learning tasks

Instructor resource sharing: with instructors collaborating and building shared curriculum archives in ways not possible before

Enhanced communication: instructor–student, student–student

Global access: to learners and to instructors

Why Use E-Learning?

In today's fast-paced world, it is necessary to find alternatives to the typical face-to-face teaching of the twentieth century. A number of reasons have influenced the library world to embrace different training methods. Library schools, such as San Jose State University and Drexel University, offer master of library and information science programs totally online. Others use a blended approach, with classroom and online sessions. Businesses can provide more training at lower cost using online instruction, and public libraries or organizations, including the Public Library Association and state libraries, can reach more librarians with it, especially those in small and rural libraries, where staff is not always available to free the librarian for staff development travel.

Advantages and Disadvantages of Webinars for a Library and Its Patrons

As learning and education continue to evolve, the distinctions among teaching techniques are quickly becoming difficult to detect. New technology has also eliminated some of the obstacles to early distance instruction. As you consider whether e-learning is the right choice for your audience, evaluate what you want to impart to a group of students, what their readiness is (and yours) to use different tools, what your budget is, and what your technical resources and knowledge are. Then examine all the potential options to create the right combination of interaction, presentation, teamwork, research, creative thinking, response, and feedback. You may find a combination that feels right and comfortable for many kinds of teaching situations, or you may have to use a variety of types of instruction. Either way, online instruction is one of those to consider.

Because an instruction librarian's goal is to make instruction more creative, personalized, hands-on, meaningful, and effective for the participants, it is necessary to consider advantages and challenges of e-learning for the library and its patrons.

Benefits of Online Learning

Distance, time, and technology are all factors. Online seminars, or webinars, are a dynamic and engaging way to convey information to a geographically dispersed audience on a budget. If your nonprofit public library faces an ongoing need to share information long-distance but has limited education and travel funds, webinars can help you save money while providing a valuable service to your patrons.

One major advantage of online learning is its convenience and portability. Because courses do not require physical attendance, they are accessible 24/7 on one's own schedule. A synchronous environment also approximates the visual and audio stimulation of a classroom so that participants can see and hear one another even though they are geographically separated. Some of these systems can be accessed with a cell phone or tablet computer, making it extremely portable. Online features such as chat, questions, and polling enhance presentational sessions so that interactivity and collaboration are much easier among students. The tools also facilitate linking and integrating nontext content into the discussion. Using breakout rooms offers quick one-on-one updates, and just-in-time coaching is available. Finally, students who tend to hang back in face-to-face discussions are encouraged to participate in this virtual environment. They have the time to think through their responses before deciding to answer.

In addition, materials can be downloaded before, during, or after a session. Curriculum consistency is maintained over time. Archives of all contributions are automatically available for later viewing and review, making it easier to evaluate on the basis of what actually took place (rather than your recollection of what took place) and allowing search and sort by date, contributor, topic, and so on.

As a result of the economic downturn and less funding, all libraries are looking for ways to conserve money but still provide a diverse selection of training options for their patrons. Web-based training can meet both goals. Although online training may have more up-front costs, the web-based equipment can be reused. A wide range of prices fits most budgets. With little bandwidth and low-end computers, access—particularly global access—is more equitable. Online instruction can offer versatile goals to meet different needs, whether patrons need to get a degree, acquire a new skill, or learn a new craft. Such instruction can simulate many work situations, provide practice in real time, monitor progress, and measure and document improvements.

Online learning is also flexible. Instruction can be created to accommodate student preferences and needs; patrons can choose instructor-led courses or self-study courses without an instructor. A wide range of tools suits patrons' learning styles. Moreover, learning with the same instructor is available to the global learning community despite differences in time zones and distant locations. Instruction is not bound by place; students can study at home, at work, or on the road.

Challenges of Online Learning

Webinars are used for a variety of purposes, including software training, sharing information about a new service, or promoting a program. Moreover, new online tools are making it easy for any organization to host a webinar, even with limited technological expertise. However, there are challenges that must be faced and considered before implementing online instruction. Specifically, online programs

- are complex in terms of running all the pieces at the same time, including sign-up, question monitoring, chat, and participant supervising in various activities;
- usually require local software installations, which can be difficult or impossible for some students, depending on information technology requirements;
- depend on well-planned and well-executed instruction so that participants do not multitask during the session;
- need strong writing and planning skills to avoid typos, ignorance of grammar rules, attempts at humor that go awry, and so on; and
- demand scrutiny of resource material to prevent overload.

Who Should Take Online Classes

E-learning courses are a great option for students who might have difficulty attending classes on campus, those who enjoy alternative learning environments, seniors or the disabled who cannot always get to the library, and patrons of corporate libraries who are often widely dispersed. However, being successful in most e-learning courses requires skills that participants may not anticipate. A level of self-discipline, motivation, and commitment is necessary, as is self-direction, effective time management, and independent problem solving. Finally, online students must also be able to stay on task.

Because online courses are delivered at a distance, they are reading and writing intensive. For example, an academic institution may host a synchronous class, where attendance is required for all at a specific time, or it may host an asynchronous session, where participants work at their own pace, on their own schedule. Either way, students will need to spend time in the virtual classroom five out of every seven days and plan on twelve to fifteen hours of class work each week for each course, just as they would in a face-to-face classroom.

The reasons for introducing technology into the learning environment and the purpose that it is intended to serve need to be carefully considered and articulated as part of the planning of an online or blended class. Although technology becomes easier to use all the time, e-learning courses do require a minimum level of computer competency. Participants in online classes may need the following competencies, depending on the instruction offered:

- Having comfort with computers that meet the technical requirements of the e-learning class or session
- Knowing how to connect to the Internet using a browser such as Internet Explorer, Chrome, or Firefox

- Navigating the web and using search engines such as Google or Yahoo
- Working with a variety of computer applications, including e-mail; saving, copying, and opening documents; and having basic word-processing skills, such as cutting and pasting
- Managing and organizing files
- Having access to a computer five to seven days per week

Of primary importance when beginning to plan an online class is to realize that technology will not automatically bring benefits and solve any existing curriculum problems for the instructor without rethinking the pedagogy. In other words, the introduction of an online component will not automatically make a class or program more relevant to today's students and is not a guarantee of increasing student engagement. Merely taking one's existing face-to-face content and teaching strategies will not necessarily work as effectively in an online environment without some adjustment or planning. The instructor must also consider that digital natives—those growing up with the Internet—may not be familiar with technology as a teaching tool, so digital literacy instruction may be necessary. Finally, if assessment is involved, one must align it with the learning outcomes of the online session.

Instructor as Facilitator

Today's instruction librarian must learn to be more of a facilitator. Interaction has become all important. Key components of an online facilitator are to

- engage learners by creating a learner-led environment, give and receive feedback from participants, and handle any challenging situations that occur;
- use a variety of delivery strategies to present and build knowledge and increase participant confidence;
- incorporate instructional design principles to design and organize learning experiences that bring learning alive and focus on outcomes;
- use motivating, diverse teaching aids;
- self-assess participant performance as the lesson progresses;
- share lessons learned and best practices; and
- incorporate technology as a component that enhances the learning and teaching experience and is carefully integrated into the curriculum planning.

Synchronous vs. Asynchronous Instruction

The delivery method is the medium through which course content is transmitted and human interaction occurs. The choice of delivery method is influenced by a number of factors, which include the nature of the content, the characteristics of the learner, the specific environments for learning, and the available technologies. Delivery methods fall under two broad areas: synchronous and asynchronous.

Synchronous e-learning events happen in real time—bringing instructor and student together at the same time in a live online event. It involves social learning principles and dynamics, whether the interaction is one-to-one, one-to-many, or many-to-many. For example, an academic class or a company webinar is usually a real-time, moderated online learning event in which all participants are available at the same time and can communicate directly with one another.

Synchronous methodology provides immediate availability of the instructor for questions and feedback. It offers many types of tools, is similar to the classroom, and allows for real-time collaboration among participants. Features include

- live interaction in real time;
- individual and group work;
- presentation formats for discussion and lecture;
- input from the instructor, guest speakers, and other students;
- resource tools and materials that can be introduced, presented, and shared;
- student activity that can be monitored and facilitated by the instructor.

Asynchronous learning is self-paced—occurring at different times as determined by the learners. In asynchronous e-learning, participants (learners and instructors) are not online at the same time. This type of instruction is often referred to as *self-paced* or *self-directed learning*. Self-managing learning events are how adult learners prefer to learn. Most important, asynchronous learning offers the dramatic economic impact of making curriculum available 24/7. The essential dialogue of an instructor–student relationship can still be preserved in a self-paced distance model if the tutorial is designed to include person-to-person contact through e-mail, threaded discussion, phone, and/or video. Interaction can also occur with media tools, such as chat and social media (e.g., Twitter, blogs, and wikis), which allow learners to communicate with their peers, instructors, experts, and so on. While these types of social media are not quite as synchronous as face-to-face or live chats, they do create a close approximation if they are supported properly. However, many academic institutions and public libraries lack the necessary resources to build e-learning content to either offer complete courses online or supplement classroom courses.

Clark and Mayer (2011), in their book *E-Learning and the Science of Instruction: Proven Guidelines for Consumers and Designers of Multimedia Learning*, cite studies indicating that, based on achieving learning outcomes, there is no difference between face-to-face and online instruction. The authors comment on four factors that may determine which approach to use: pacing, timing, the permanent nature of the content, and peer interaction.

If learners need to review the material more than once—perhaps it is complex or the audience is totally unfamiliar with the content—self-paced material may be the better choice. Self-paced material requires no physical boundaries. It can be completed anytime, anywhere. For example, a course where the purpose is annual compliance, such as updating a real estate credential, a deadline is set, and all participants must complete the course by the deadline. Live courses would take longer and be more expensive to conduct and finish.

Another factor must be considered: permanence of content. If the content does not change over time, a self-paced video or tutorial would suffice. However, if the content is continually changing, it is easier to update a live session than a self-paced one, especially if the tutorial has been created outside the library. For example, if you are creating how-to instruction on a software package and the software is often updated, you will spend a lot of time and money to keep the tutorial current.

Also important for learning is interactivity. If a learner using self-paced instruction needs to clarify a concept in a tutorial, it is necessary to have a method of communicating with the instructor or other participants in a timely manner. With live online instruction, a simple question in the chat can offer the answer quickly. Also, learning from one another is especially important to adult learners. A blended approach or a flipped approach could take advantage of the benefits of both methods. In a flipped class, you can use videos, for example, to deliver lectures or provide uncomplicated material *before* a presentation and save higher-level discussion for the live portion of the session (hence, flipped). Chapter 7 discusses variations of web-based synchronous instruction. Chapter 8 focuses on asynchronous training, types and materials, and how to create them.

Synchronous Instruction

Sophisticated technology has removed many of the barriers to online instruction so that similar teaching strategies can be used. A 2011 Kaplan study (Bullmaster-Day 2011) indicated that online or blended learning courses usually include some mix of three kinds of instruction:

- direct presentation of material through lecture, text, visuals, and animation;
- active learning where the individual student researches information, solves problems, takes quizzes, and engages in drills, simulations, or games; and
- interactive learning, where students collaborate with other students.

The study concluded that effective online and blended learning must be personalized and adaptive to meet individual learning needs. It should also support high levels of critical thinking to meet learning objectives, and it should balance computer- or teacher-led guidance with learner control.

The following sections outline different types of instruction that provide librarians with the opportunity to participate in online instruction.

Librarian-Led Online Information Literacy Course

The best way to ensure that students receive the necessary education to become information-literate, lifelong learners is to have a class that all students must successfully complete to continue their studies. In a semester course, librarians could cover all the topics that are so often missed with one-shot library instruction classes, such as evaluating sources and information on the Internet, successful searching, transferring skills across the disciplines, citing sources, avoiding plagiarism, and understanding copyright laws.

One of the many advantages experienced by one librarian of an online information literacy course is that by teaching the students the limits of Internet search engines, they become encouraged to use resources such as electronic databases and other library sources. This class's assignments also required the students to experience realistic information-seeking processes, wherein it might not always be easy to find the answer. This is often better than leading students through canned searches. This training teaches them how to formulate searches and where to go for help when difficulties arise.

Blended Instruction

The term *blended learning* refers to courses that combine face-to-face classroom instruction with online learning and reduced classroom contact hours. Blended learning combines the effectiveness and socialization opportunities of the classroom with the technologically enhanced active learning possibilities of the online environment. Success in a blended learning situation requires a planned and well-supported approach, high-quality faculty development, course development assistance, learner support, and ongoing assessment. Blended learning has the following characteristics:

- a shift from lecture- to student-centered instruction in which students become active and interactive learners;
- increased interaction between student and instructor, student and student, student and content, and student and outside resources; and
- integrated formative and summative assessment mechanisms for students and instruction.

Depending on the proportion of web-to-classroom time, the course may be web-enhanced classroom instruction or classroom-enhanced online instruction (Brunvand, 2004).

Embedded Librarians

An embedded librarian actually becomes a part of a class, either face-to-face or online, often as part of a library discussion forum within the class. Before the beginning of class, the instructor and the librarian determine the role that the librarian will play in the classroom. The students are informed of the librarian's presence and how to contact the librarian for assistance. If the embedded librarian has a designated discussion forum, it encourages students to post their questions online. The openness of the discussion forum allows all students to benefit from one another's questions. The librarian also has the opportunity to post information online to further assist students. Topics might include Boolean searching, evaluating resources, citing sources, avoiding plagiarism, help with specific assignments, and so on. Furthermore, a shy or nervous student can benefit from reading other students' questions and answers without having to build the nerve to ask questions on his or her own. The disadvantage here is the time commitment. Embedded librarians must decide how much time they can commit aside from their other library responsibilities.

Concentrate on the important questions of instructional design and effective methodology. Understanding the learner and the process of organizing instruction are the critical issues. Accommodate the individual by tailoring instruction to his or her needs. Whether the instruction is totally online and given solely by the librarian, a mix of classroom and online instruction created and presented by a faculty member and a librarian, or an online or classroom course where the proportion of teaching is handled equally by teacher and librarian, it is important to find a combination of instructional methods that feels right and comfortable for your teaching situation. That said, even though the course topic and goals may be the same as in a face-to-face course, the course layout, pacing, content delivery, and assignments will all be tailored for online delivery.

Examples of Synchronous Online Learning

With more sophisticated, easy-to-use technology tools, all types of libraries—academic, public, and special—are offering online instruction. Online workshops, webinars, blended instruction, and embedded librarianship are all illustrations of live online instruction. The examples that follow illustrate how academic and public libraries are using this training.

Example 1: Academic Library Blended Learning

The University of Central Florida offers a continuum of instructional models ranging from fully face-to-face to completely online. Between the two are blended courses. In the words of many faculty members, blended instruction provides the "best of both worlds." A benefit, not often mentioned, is the resulting increase in student information literacy, providing students with new abilities that help them throughout their entire academic and employment careers. In blended courses, the university has found high levels of student and faculty satisfaction, student learning outcomes that are higher than those in comparable face-to-face and fully online courses, and high student demand because of the increased convenience and flexibility. Two challenges that the school is facing are, first, the demand for multimedia-equipped classrooms that may exceed the supply and, second, classroom scheduling. Review more about the University of Central Florida's online program at http://teach.ucf.edu/2011/11/01/engaging-online-students-practical-interaction-strategies-to-enhance-learning/.

Example 2: In-Service Online Workshops

Faculty workshops may be targeted to specific audiences such as distance faculty, as noted by Miller et al. (2010). At the University of Maryland University College, librarians have taken a slightly different approach to the in-service model by presenting synchronous online workshops lasting seven to twelve days that introduce distance faculty to the library. These sessions are cofacilitated by a librarian and the academic director of a given department, but content is created solely by the library. The Miller et al. article includes detailed descriptions of the workshops that are likely to be useful for anyone considering a similar approach.

Example 3: Virtual Academic Information Literacy Course

Information literacy initiatives have been started in numerous departments across the University of Texas at Austin. Librarians have created the Signature Course Faculty Toolkit to provide faculty with resources to generate keywords for a research topic, learn about plagiarism, understand citations, and more. These tools help faculty incorporate library research into their class projects and use the library more effectively. For example, the university integrates web-based online information literacy instruction tutorials into first-year college courses to enhance students' conceptual grasp of information resource selection, database searching, and Internet source evaluation (see http://www.lib.utexas.edu/signaturecourses/topic?tid=775).

Creating Synchronous E-Learning Lessons

How to undertake research in general is a common topic that can be a course of its own or one integrated into many disciplines. Either way, it can take the form of web-based tutorials, especially for distance education students who are not able to receive face-to-face instruction. Typical topics covered include planning research, identifying and refining a topic, using the online catalog, evaluating information, citing resources, and differentiating among types of resources.

Although some may think that using the Internet is too commonplace a topic, many people still seek instruction on how to access and use it. The elderly especially turn to the public library to learn the basics of the Internet. Highlighting features and functions of browsers is one; online communication is another, especially e-mail, discussion groups, blogging, and social networking. There will continue to be a need to instruct people on the use of web search tools or how to conduct a search so that the amount of information they retrieve is not overwhelming. Teaching students to evaluate web resources is all important with the myriad sources available to them.

The amount of time that it takes to meet your objectives and cover the subject may not be suited to online learning. Most online audiences tend to lose interest after about an hour, so you need to organize topics and information that can be adequately covered within a given time constraint. Also, think whether you can break your material into chunks or provide a series of sessions over a longer period. Informal conversations, formal interviews, surveys, and polls can all help you assess whether a webinar is the right medium for your audience's needs.

Tips for Designing Synchronous Instruction

The default mode of communicating course content—the lecture—is generally absent or minimal in an online course. Think of this as liberating rather than constraining, as there are many means to deliver content. Take what the learners need to "know" and put that content in a self-directed e-learning module; then give the learners the opportunity to practice what they need to "do" in a face-to-face synchronous environment. Some tips will help you enhance your instruction:

- Design for interaction, collaboration, and contribution.
- Count on the first session taking fifteen minutes to kick off, especially if people are new to the technique. Build that time into the first presentation. Also, have a technical person on standby to troubleshoot anything from the presenter's end.
- At the beginning of the session, schedule up to ten minutes of time with a specific activity to let participants try out collaboration and annotation tools to get comfortable with them so that participation is easy.
- To set interaction expectations early, poll, survey, or use some other activity within the first five to ten minutes of your web-based training session. Follow up with additional activities every fifteen to twenty minutes. You may do polls and surveys via your web meeting tool or, if your group is small, verbally. Be sure to share the poll or survey results with your web attendees.
- Keep the content visually engaging but not too busy. If using PowerPoint, consider the animation tool to provide more dynamic content by emphasizing what you are discussing, especially steps in a process.
- Use a whiteboard or blank PowerPoint slide to brainstorm ideas on a topic, rather than presenting them with bulleted lists. Allow participants to type directly in the space, if possible, or write their inputs.
- Design opportunities to use feedback mechanisms to get *yes/no*, *agree/disagree*, and *like/dislike* reactions from participants and respond to the feedback.
- Make sure that you outline your course. A table of contents and flow of the course will typically be like an outline. It presets and guides you during creation and verifies that you cover all topics.

- Use appropriate, consistent, teachable images rather than bulleted lists.
- Avoid wireless network connections to prevent intermittent lapses that can happen with even the best wireless connection.
- Try presenting information in the form of an activity. You do not have to present content in a lecture and then review it in an activity. Review as you go. For example, you can present information in an activity and review it in another activity or in a lecture format. That way, you can build in more interaction, and you can get your participants thinking about the content while it is being presented.
- Design the assessments from the start as you are working up your overall course design. This allows the assignments to be integrated within the course rather than tacked on top of the course content.
- Practice before the live event. Upload content, walk through exercises, conduct polls, and so on. Going through your session at least once, before you have your participants, will allow you to identify areas of concern and find solutions.
- For training that is one day or longer, use a team-teaching approach whenever possible. It will help the students stay attentive when they have a variety of voices and presentation styles to listen to during the session. Here is where the faculty member and librarian partnership makes a real difference.
- Develop a communication plan so that you maintain constant communication with learners, before and during learning sessions. Follow up a webinar event with refresher information or activities that require the attendees to recall or apply what they have learned.

An effective synchronous session may build on several hours of asynchronous preparation and provide the stimulus for several hours of follow-up. Use the asynchronous environments to distribute information prior to the session (e.g., web documents to read, videos to watch, slideshows to view, podcasts to listen to), and use the valuable time of the synchronous session to discuss, debate, and clarify the material and develop the understandings that are required.

Keep in mind that, with a little creativity, you can convert almost all classroom exercises to a synchronous online format. Learn how to use all the tools in your synchronous package—and then actually use them! Groups can work on a section of a whiteboard while they chat with one another, or they can go to a breakout room.

Asynchronous Instruction

Self-directed methods of instruction are becoming increasingly popular as the education world shifts from the classroom to the Internet. Librarians have been creating self-directed learning materials for years. Today, however, more classes, workshops, and individualized materials are created for online use. Some instruction librarians are already meeting this challenge.

Examples of Asynchronous, Self-Directed Learning

Self-paced, self-directed materials are on the rise. They range from videos to printed materials to e-learning courses. Many libraries are creating them, and those in electronic format have become quite popular. The following examples demonstrate how libraries are implementing e-learning courses and how these and other self-paced materials can enhance teaching and learning.

Example 1: Shoreline Community College Library Technology Center

Shoreline Community College has continued to develop self-paced tools (http://ww2.shoreline.edu/library/docs/newsletter.9.10.pdf). Tutorials created with Camtasia (easy-to-use software) are being used for library orientation. They can be used as homework, with quizzes, as introductions to research workshops with a librarian, and to supplement course LibGuides and research tutorials. LibGuides have been created as course guides to be used with their learning management system's (Blackboard) online courses. Social media using Facebook and Twitter feeds helps to connect with students through tips on the research process and information literacy. You will learn more about these resources in chapter 8.

Example 2: Academic Self-Directed Tutorial

The University of Saskatchewan introduced a new graduate course incorporating screencast tutorials to help students learn strategies to proficiently complete systematic literature reviews. While the tutorials were generally well received by the class, assessment activities (e.g., student observation, process assignments, and interviews) revealed that students did not fully understand the literature search process. Two problems emerged: first, students had trouble understanding the information in the tutorials; second, some tutorials had incomplete information. Using Bloom's taxonomy knowledge dimension (factual, conceptual, and procedural knowledge) along with the cognitive process dimension (remember, understand, apply, analyze, evaluate, and create), the creators of the online tutorials added more exercises to promote critical thinking skills. A knowledge gap was noted between older students just coming back to academia and younger, native Internet users. Consequently, the authors recommended conducting an initial assessment of incoming students' skill levels using online library resources and tailoring instruction based on students' needs.

Example 3: Public Library Online Course

The Matteson Public Library (Illinois) adheres to the concept of lifelong learning. Matteson offers a range of online continuing education courses, from medicine to homeschooling to computer skills and more. Patrons can enroll in up to five courses with access 24/7 via the Internet. Other opportunities include courses to learn a new language and the Learning Express Library, with tutorials and materials for subjects such as GED preparation, jobs and careers, and U.S. citizenship, to name a few. This comprehensive offering provides learning for all age groups on subjects that patrons need most, and because courses are all online, patrons can attend anytime from anywhere. Many of these courses are made available through partnerships with other organizations.

Creating Asynchronous, Self-Paced Instruction

Because asynchronous material must be created almost entirely prior to its use, establishing a framework for content, structure, delivery, and assessment must be considered before developing your online self-directed instruction, whatever form it might take. The following steps will get you started.

Step 1: Consider the Design

A variety of self-paced training materials have potential for learning, depending on the needs of the patrons who will use them. Design, audience, type of material, and purpose must be well thought out before creation of the actual tool. It is more important to get it right the first time than in a face-to-face class or a synchronous session, which can be changed on the fly.

Create an outline by answering the following questions:

- Initial considerations concern patron requirements, the scope of the project, and the need that the resource is supposed to fulfill—ask yourself, what is the project about? who is involved? and what will your role be?
- What type of self-paced material will you create? Many choices exist for this type of instruction: video, podcast/audio, search aids, LibGuides, fact sheets—the list goes on.
- Who is the audience? You will need to consider the course attendees—how much do they know about the subject? what method will provide the most effective coverage of the topic? how much prior knowledge do they have? and what other resources can they use if they need more help? Also important are personal characteristics: age, language ability, special needs, educational level, and computer skills, to name a few.
- What do you want to achieve? What are the objectives of the instruction? How do you determine the success of your project? How do you measure success?

These questions and their characteristics may sound familiar to any instructor; however, the important difference is that the e-learning material must be completed before its use. It cannot be immediately adapted to meet the needs of its users. Once you have answered these questions, you are ready to begin to develop, test, and deliver e-learning material.

Step 2: Assess Needs to Develop the Content

Set priorities for the content to be developed. Determine what content is most important to your patrons. Numerous libraries survey their patrons to find out some of the most important topics for potential online instruction. You might consider doing the same at your library. Resources are usually limited, so not every need can be fulfilled. The San Francisco City Survey, which includes the public library, is completed yearly and suggests some of the most important topics for potential online instruction:

Library skills, including database and catalog: 64.6 percent of those likely to use online instruction selected "Finding useful articles or information through databases" and 36.5 percent selected "Using the library catalog."

Employment skills: 45 percent of respondents were also more likely to be unemployed and looking for work. Allot time for staff to support employment needs in a one-to-one setting, and expand classroom training to include additional research, database, and library usage skills training.

Step 3: Decide on the Content of the Self-Paced Course or Material

The recent increased demand for library services and simultaneous decrease in funding brought on by the recession highlight a need for innovative, low-cost, high-impact information services such as online patron instruction. It is important to provide topics that meet the needs of library patrons—students who need to use the online library catalogue, unemployed persons who cannot write a resume, teens who want help with their homework, and seniors who want to learn about e-mail. Libraries can provide a wealth of subjects, but they must decide how many resources they can create, what in-house expertise they have, and what budget and time they have to fill the need.

Areas of instruction requested include the following:

Content areas: Content most often cited by patrons and by library staff included, in order of frequency,

Employment issues—job seeking, resume writing, and completion of online job applications

Social service and government needs—access to outside resources such as ESL (English as a second language) classes, immigration appointments, youth programs, food assistance, tax help, legal information

Educational needs—homework help, research needs, information on schools and colleges

Business needs—directories, research, small business development

Other issues—including personal enrichment, recreation, and home and garden.

Skills-based needs: Mentioned significantly more often than content-specific needs were skills, which centered on three areas:

General computer skills—including basic skills, such as accessing and navigating the Internet, using e-mail, and typing, and intermediate skills, such as uploading and downloading files, scanning photographs, social networking, and using other Internet-based tools (e.g., Google Docs)

Library usage skills—including knowledge of library services, materials, and programs; use of library technology, including basic skills such as using the catalog to search, printing at the library, using an e-reader and checking out e-books, and using the self checkout machines; and intermediate skills, including advanced catalog searches and database searching

Employment skills—including searching for jobs online, resume writing, interviewing, and completing online job applications

Social services: citizenship, housing, immigration appointments, tax information, government information, ESL classes and materials

Business and consumer needs: small business work, real estate, and directories

Education and research needs: locating schools or colleges, determining courses offered, finishing homework.

Depending on the library's geographic location and population size (urban vs. rural), the needs of patrons may vary.

Step 4: Outline the Content

Write an outline of the content for the self-paced resource. Perhaps fill in some ideas concerning details. Some people prefer to organize with maps or graphical outlines instead of text. Others use notes of their ideas as a sketch of the instructional aid.

Draw a map of how the various parts of the tutorial or video will fit together. In some cases, it will be straightforward, but other materials may have many twists and turns, as with a game. The map gives you the viewpoint of the resource as it flows from beginning to end. This map will be your guide to setting up the navigation through your computer- or web-based tutorial. Ask yourself, "If the user gets sidetracked, how does he or she get back on course?" Remember that you will not be guiding the learner's every move, so the resource must be able to stand on its own.

Step 5: Select Learner Activities

Consider activities and exercises to enhance the learning of the material. Are there multiple-choice questions? Do the students play games or solve puzzles? Are there simulations of real activities? Think in terms of education while keeping the learner interested in the material. Try not to get into entertainment for its own sake. The purpose of the e-learning is training, not amusement.

Write a short essay that defines what the self-directed course or tutorial is all about. What is its purpose? What does the user have to do? How can you tell if the instructional material is effective? If you cannot explain it, then you cannot sell it to the learners.

Step 6: Storyboard How the Course Will Look

Take the material to be learned and sketch how it will look on the screen. This can be done on a series of sheets of paper or cards that can be laid out according to your map. If any multimedia effects are to be used, you can produce them to insert into the program at the appropriate locations. This can include graphics, illustrations, animations, sound effects, music, voice, and video, according to your objectives for the topic. You may have to use graphical artists and multimedia experts to assist in this area. Of course, the delivery medium affects the type of multimedia that is practical.

Step 7: Use Software to Create the Material

Actually write and program the course, with authoring software. You may have to work in coordination with an instructional designer. Test it to make sure it works correctly. See chapter 8 for more details.

Step 8: Evaluate the Course

Try out the material on other librarians or patrons to make sure that the objectives are met. Try to get some honest feedback. See where learners might be confused. You can use a survey, but verbal feedback from learners is best. Evaluate the results and make appropriate changes. Ask yourself the following:

- Is there a clear objective to the training session?
- Is it easy to use and understand?

- Can you go through it at your own pace, or are you controlled by the program?
- Is it boring? Too simple? Too difficult?

Note: Users may become bored with your e-learning. Use methods to relieve boredom, such as emphasizing value, providing moderate interaction, and allowing some entertainment in the session.

⑥ Key Points

More librarian job descriptions call for teaching as a desired skill. Instruction librarians who coteach or participate in blended instruction are now a vital part of a library's resources. Technology provides ways of efficiently and effectively storing and delivering these instructional messages; however, the technology itself does not directly affect learning. Rather, educational technology can facilitate the teaching and learning process and potentially make education richer and more stimulating by creating environments and presenting content not possible otherwise. No matter whether the librarian is creating synchronous or asynchronous instruction, understanding the learner and organizing the training and materials are critical issues for librarians. The instruction librarian's task is to tailor instruction to individual learner needs and discover the most effective means of using technology to facilitate learning for all.

Table 6.1. URLs for Chapter 6

DESCRIPTION	URL
Virginia Commonwealth pilot online library training	http://www.sla.org/pdfs/sla2007/kirlewonlinelibinstrsvcs.pdf
Small public library program to instruct job hunters on computer basics	http://www.webjunction.org/resources/WebJunction/Documents/webjunction/Project%20Compass%20Workbook_04.12.pdf
Videos on topics such as computer basic skills	http://pascolibraries.org/egovtools.shtml
Workforce services	http://www.webjunction.org/explore-topics/workforce-resources/materials.html
Website with examples of embedded librarians	http://embeddedlibrarian.com
How to videos for tech basics, web, communication, media	http://www.teachparentstech.org/watch
ADDIE video	http://www.youtube.com/watch?v=jiLLz1SaxGc
National Survey of Patron Instruction in Public Libraries	http://www.webjunction.org/resources/WebJunction/Documents/webjunction/Project%20Compass%2021st%20Century%20Skills%20Focus.pdf
In the Library with the Lead Pipe—Embracing Your Teacher Identity	http://www.inthelibrarywiththeleadpipe.org/2009/sense-of-self-embracing-your-teacher-identity/
Quick check for online courses from University of Central Florida	http://teach.ucf.edu/2013/04/04/tune-up-your-course-with-the-online-course-quick-check/

Note. ADDIE = analysis, design, development, implementation, evaluation.

Completing the following exercises will reinforce what you learned in this chapter.

1. Based on what you read in the chapter and your prior knowledge, list attributes that a good facilitator might need. Include personal and professional attributes.
2. Read the following scenario and answer the questions about the facilitator and her methodology for teaching the class.

Jane is the facilitator of an online session. The session used activities to focus on the learners that allowed them to interact with the content and share ideas with one another. Jane took a keen interest in understanding the participants' contexts, and she provided feedback accordingly. Through interactive strategies such as brainstorming and discussion sessions, Jane engaged the learners as a class and in groups. Moreover, she allowed learners the opportunity to interact with the content by designing web-based instructional projects. This personalized instruction engaged the participants. At the end of the session, each attendee left the workshop with a unit of web-based instruction created during the session. Jane also used multiple methods of presenting content and engaging the learners so that they were motivated, and she maintained their attention throughout the online session.

3. Based on the scenario, add attributes of a good facilitator to your list. Which are most common? Which appear only once? Prioritize the attributes. Are there any attributes listed that you disagree with?
4. Take this online quiz at http://www.waol.org/prospective_students/isOnLineForMe .aspx to find out if you are ready to take online classes.

References

Brunvand, Amy. 2004. "Integrating Library Reference Services in an Online Information Literacy Course: The Internet Navigator as a Model." *Internet Reference Services Quarterly* 9:159–77.

Bullmaster-Day, Marcella. 2011. "Online and Blended Learning: What the Research Says." White paper. New York: Kaplan K12 Learning Services.

Clark, R. C., and R. E. Mayer. 2011. *E-Learning and the Science of Instruction: Proven Guidelines for Consumers and Designers of Multimedia Learning*. San Francisco: Pfeiffer.

Institute of Museum and Library Services. 2009. *Museums, Libraries, and 21st Century Skills* (IMLS-2009-NAI-01). Washington, DC: Institute of Museum and Library Services.

Miller, R., E. O'Donnell, N. Pomea, J. Rawson, R. Shepard, and C. Thomes. 2010. "Library-Led Faculty Workshops: Helping Distance Educators Meet Information Literacy Goals in the Online Classroom." *Journal of Library Administration* 50 (7/8): 830–56.

⑥ Further Reading

Dziuban, Charles D., Joel L. Hartman, and Patsy D. Miskual. 2004. "Blended Learning." *Research Bulletin* 7 (March 30). University of Central Florida, Center for Applied Research. http://net .educause.edu/ir/library/pdf/erb0407.pdf.

Fabry, D. L. 2009. "Designing Online and On-Ground Courses to Ensure Comparability and Consistency in Meeting Learning Outcomes." *Quarterly Review of Distance Education* 10 (3): 253–61.

Marzano, R. J. 2007. *The Art and Science of Teaching*. Alexandria, VA: ASCD.

Morgan, Kendra. 2009. "Patron Instruction Survey Results." WebJunction and the San Francisco Public Library. http://www.webjunction.org/documents/webjunction/Patron_Instruction_ Survey_Results.html.

Mounce, M. 2010. "Working Together: Academic Librarians and Faculty Collaborating to Improve Students' Information Literacy Skills. A Literature Review 2000–2009." *Reference Librarian* 51 (4): 300–320.

Pritchard, Peggy A. 2010. "The Embedded Science Librarian: Partner in Curriculum Design and Delivery." *Journal of Library Administration* 50 (4): 373–96.

Staker, H. 2011. *The Rise of K–12 Blended Learning: Profiles of Emerging Models*. Mountain View, CA: Innosight Institute.

Varvel, V. E., Jr. 2002. "Ice-Breakers." *Pointer and Clickers: ION's Technology Tip of the Month*, 4 (1). http://www.ion.uillinois.edu/resources/pointersclickers/2002_01/index.asp.

CHAPTER 7

Synchronous Instruction

OBJECTIVES

After completing this chapter, you will be able to

▷ Explain the differences among webinar platforms

▷ Describe how to encourage audience participation and interaction in online courses

▷ Plan an online training session

▷ Create a lesson plan for online instruction

A S MORE organizations are discovering the advantages of e-learning, there is a greater push to take instructor-led courses online. Online learning is different in many respects from traditional face-to-face learning, primarily in the way that students get their information and how they interact with instructors and classmates. Many people say that they learn more online and that their retention is better too.

The challenge, of course, is how to do this effectively. If libraries want to remain relevant and vital to their communities, they need to reach out to their users in virtual and physical spaces beyond the traditional library walls. Library instruction is no different. It needs to go beyond the traditional library classroom with twenty computers and a whiteboard.

Instruction librarians must acknowledge the fact that online learning is different in many respects from traditional face-to-face learning and emphasize those differences when they create their own synchronous instruction.

Student and library patron comments emphasize how they want to learn. They want to experience the concepts they've been exploring through reading; they need to be able to actually do the tasks, not just answer questions about them on an exam. Although students and library patrons may not express these ideas in writing, most want more from a course presentation or workshop than readings and tests. They expect to be able to perform, create, and apply the knowledge and skills. Consider how you can address outcomes through meaningful sets of learning experiences. For example, what activities can you offer patrons in public libraries who want to create a resume? What tasks will show students how to create a search strategy or seniors learn basic computer skills? To use the information they learn, they must practice it in library sessions and continue to reinforce what they learned outside the library through follow-up activities

This chapter reviews important issues surrounding the use of live e-learning. It compares and contrasts some of the most-used online learning formats. Examples illustrate libraries that are conducting live online training. Finally, it reviews lesson plans created as models for use in academic and special libraries.

⊚ Characteristics of Successful Webinars

A multidimensional approach is necessary to serve all students. To create and deliver engaging, successful webinars and other components of a virtual classroom, master the following.

Make the Webinar Collaboration Engaging, Interactive, and Fun

One of the most important aspects of online learning is engaging students. Web conference technologies offer numerous different ways for e-learners to interact; thus, it is important to identify the tools of a system and use them to meet your objectives and teach your content.

A web-based package usually includes screen sharing, integrated voice conferencing, and recording capabilities for later listening, participant polling, managing questions, and text chat functions. Some systems also include collaborative capabilities to enhance teamwork among dispersed students, such as a shared whiteboard and breakout rooms. Links to other resources and readings, as well as library or online resource connections, are often available. Most systems support multiple presenters where they can pass the control of the session to one another. Other tools provide the ability to manage registrations, automatically e-mail reminders before an event or class, and send follow-up materials after an event, as well as conduct postevent reporting on participation levels and interactions during the session (e.g., questions asked, attentiveness to the screen during live sessions).

Instructors can collect responses to given discussion topics and distribute them automatically via e-mail to class participants, turning a "pull" communication (one that a user has to go out and get) into a "push" communication (one that a user receives directly).

Train Instructors to Drive Vigorous, Relevant Interaction

Instructors need training to be able to leverage their web conference technology to drive relevant interaction throughout the webinar. To keep e-learners engaged, you will need changes in interaction activities about every seven minutes.

Train Designers to Reformat for Online Instruction and Then Build In Relevant Interaction Throughout

Online learners want a very different course than do face-to-face learners. Designers need training in how to redesign the course so that it will actively engage a virtual learner.

They need to build in numerous changes in interactive activities into the e-learning playbook. Ideas to be considered include audio files, video, discussions, and interactive tutorials as part of the lessons. In these forums, there are many opportunities to incorporate active, collaborative learning and use multimedia to enhance instruction. Chat options are available as part of online learning systems. Many synchronous chat systems can now be accessed with a cell phone or tablet computer, making it an extremely portable tool. Focused team projects, quick one-on-one updates, and just-in-time coaching can also be achieved online. Synchronous chat is also integrated into Google (Google Chat and Google Voice), Facebook, and Skype.

Blend the E-Learning, as Needed, to Suit the Content

It is easier to keep the attention of e-learners in online training by keeping sessions short—not usually more than one hour, which means that you might need to divide the instruction over several days. Blended instruction will also help motivate the learners. Using both online and face-to-face instruction will help maintain learners' attention. When blending the media for a virtual classroom, choose the best media for the content and the audience.

Leverage Video

In webinars, one way to establish and build rapport is to use video to show the presenter so that he or she seems to have eye contact with the audience. Turn it on only at selected times during the session—for example, when you open the session or are facilitating a discussion. When using YouTube videos, keep them short, high value, relevant, and scripted.

Make Audio Clear

Use a headset with a microphone and a wired telephone for the facilitator's audio so that the voice sounds clear and close. Encourage others to do the same. In YouTube videos, use a stereo microphone so that the voice in playback will come out of both speakers.

Obtain the Help of an Assistant (Cofacilitator, Moderator, Producer)

In a complex session, you may want to have an assistant help keep the online session running, freeing you to teach. Train the moderator to manage technical issues and provide the level of support that is needed so that the presenter can focus on facilitating the session in ways that keep learners actively engaged.

Practice Makes Perfect and Enhances Confidence

Because there are many moving parts to a web-based classroom—potentially including video, Internet access, presentation slides, Q&A, polls, and so on—rehearsal before a session is important, particularly for new instructors. Even if you have taught face-to-face instruction, you want to exhibit enthusiasm, clarity, and humor; you want to provide interaction; and you want to vary the pace and activities of the session. Someone who is dull in a live classroom can put students to sleep or encourage them to do other things in a web-based session.

◎ Creating Synchronous, E-Learning Lessons

Chapter 2 discusses the ADDIE model for creating instruction. This model is quite useful when it comes to designing effective e-learning lessons, but the design requires the same, if not more, preparation compared to classroom instruction. Since each of the two types of e-learning has its advantages, instructors often combine synchronous e-learning with classroom learning and self-paced learning.

Planning Your Online Instruction

As you join the online training world and create and deliver your first webinar, consider the following.

Step 1: Determine the Type of Instruction to Use

The decision to use webinars should be based on your objectives, the needs of your audience, and the amount of time allotted for the instruction. For example, if you are addressing a small group of patrons in a public library on how to create a resume or set up a Facebook account, a webinar may be a less appropriate option than it would be for a session in which you are teaching information literacy to a large class in an academic library. While webinars work well for some topics, they are not suited to every training need.

Step 2: Assemble Your Team

When you decide that a webinar is the right tool for you, you will need to assemble a team of staff members or volunteers to help you run the session. In general, there are three main players in a webinar: the organizer/facilitator, the presenter or presenters, and assistants. You might fill all three of these roles yourself, or you might assign them to three people, if available. The organizer is the person responsible for developing the webinar topic, locating a speaker, marketing the event, setting up the registration, and communicating with participants. During the webinar, the organizer may answer questions, monitor a chat, and encourage audience participation. The presenter should concentrate efforts on preparing any demonstration and PowerPoint slides, delivering the presentation, and fielding questions. There are at least three scenarios where you should consider having an assistant to help: first, when you or your audience is unfamiliar with webinars and webinar tools; second, when you plan to play a large role in the conversation (either as an interviewer or participant); third, when you expect a large audience. Often, assistants focus entirely on answering technical and logistical questions or introducing questions from a chat to the presenter.

Step 3: Determine the Format

The default mode of communicating course content—the lecture—is generally absent or minimal in an online course. Popular formats include one speaker, an interview format, a panel, or a totally interactive session between the speaker and the audience. The different formats depend on the number of participants, one's level of familiarity with online training, and the number of speakers and team members available.

Step 4: Plan Your Visuals

Since webinars rely on audio and visuals to get the message across, both should be engaging. Webinars should include announcement of the subject of the webinar, an introduction of presenters, and a quick overview of the session agenda. Most webinar tools allow for a variety of activities, such as shared desktop, display in real time, and interaction with programs and websites for a more dynamic presentation. Maps, charts, old photos, pictures of artifacts, paintings—all lend themselves to instructional variety. For example, if you are helping out in an American Literature class, old photos of the period in which the novel the *Grapes of Wrath* takes place would increase motivation (figure 7.1).

Web-based conferencing and webinars are commonplace tools of training today, allowing groups of individuals, all sitting at their own computers anywhere in the world, to learn and interact together. WebEx from Cisco is a common technology in corporations and businesses to transmit online instruction. Blackboard is often used in the academic field in libraries and classrooms, enabling shared screens with one or more presenters, video captures, and interactive tools, such as surveys or polls with participants. Moodle, a popular learning management system (LMS) used by the academic community, is a free web application that educators can use to create effective online learning sites. However, in practice, instructors should be aware of what corporate trainers and presenters have long known: those "participating" in a web-based conference may actually be updating their Facebook pages, reading blogs, or checking e-mail while they are logged in to the

Figure 7.1. *Grapes of Wrath* photo. *Courtesy Library of Congress.*

training session. The interactivity that you build into the session is essential for maintaining participation.

Selecting LMSs

LMS is the term used to describe a server-based system that is designed to manage learning content and learner interactions. The LMS enables the learning content to be available online, allowing participants to view and interact with learning materials through a web browser on essentially any computer—with any operating system—or even on a mobile device with browsing capability.

Many commercial LMS products are available (table 7.1). The features and functions of these systems vary considerably, but certain core functionality can be found across all of them. This includes administration features, such as student registration, course assignment, and tracking of test or quiz scores and completion status. From the student's or

Table 7.1. Learning Management Systems

PROGRAM	ADVANTAGES
Cisco WebEx[a]	
Advantages	• Delivers just-in-time internal or external online training • Reaches more people, more often, without travel, facilities, or equipment costs • Demonstrates products, concepts, and procedures using high-quality video, application sharing, threaded Q&A, and chat • Promotes critical learning skills and collaboration with virtual breakout sessions and hands-on lab • Creates a digital library of on-demand recorded lectures • Tracks attendance and training completion • Trains up to one thousand attendees at once, anywhere in the world
Disadvantage	• Does not capture scores for grading
Blackboard Collaborate[b]	
Advantages	• Connects from mobile devices or any learning management system • Communicates with two-way audio and text chat • Participates using whiteboard, application sharing, polling, feedback icons, and breakout rooms for group work • Offers powerful moderator tools • Contains interactive whiteboard and enables multiple simultaneous presenters • Shares one-on-one coaching or grants control to one or more attendees and allows them to interact with the application • Multipoint video allowing view of the speaker • Accessible to those with disabilities
Moodle[c]	
Advantages	• Offers activity modules (e.g., forums, databases, wikis) to build collaborative communities of learning • Assesses learning using assignments or quizzes

[a] http://www.webex.com/ products/elearning-and-online-training/webex-for-training.html.
[b] http://www.blackboard.com.
[c] https://moodle.org.

learner's perspective, the LMS provides personalized access to assigned course materials, messaging and notifications, and scores and transcripts.

Blackboard

Blackboard (http://www.blackboard.com) is web-based software that provides students and instructors with a set of tools to post class materials online and easily communicate with one another. Students can access the Blackboard website from anywhere they have Internet access. They can also access their online classroom from mobile devices. The Blackboard content management solution stores content in a central repository where it can be easily linked to the appropriate course. It is predominantly used by the academic community and small businesses (see figure 7.2).

Numerous tools on Blackboard are designed to enhance active learning opportunities for students:

- Course wikis, blogs and journals for collaboration on course content and group projects
- Mash-ups to integrate YouTube, Slideshare, and Flickr content
- Learning available 24/7 on mobile devices
- Learning modules with tables of contents to guide students through the learning
- Grading in parallel with review possible
- NBC News Archive available
- WIMBA for instant messaging between educators and students
- Axiom Identify-X ensuring student privacy
- Lecture-capture solution for educators to record and publish lectures

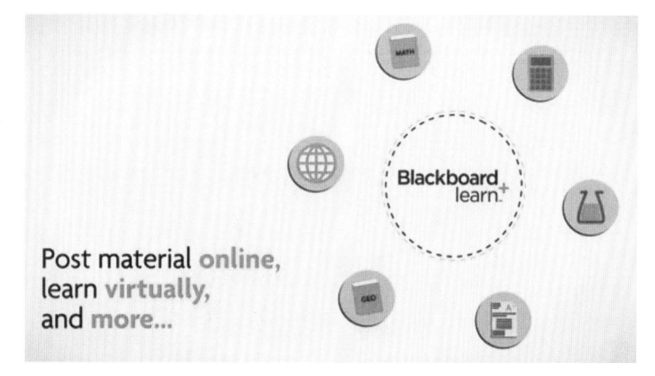

Figure 7.2. Blackboard home page.

WebEx

WebEx (http://www.webex.com) provides on-demand collaboration, online meeting and web conferencing, and videoconferencing applications, depending on the package you select. WebEx is used mostly in the corporate environment. It includes many of the features of Blackboard with the exception of a grading feature (see figure 7.3).

To use WebEx or Blackboard, you need a computer with an Internet connection and a telephone for the audio connection. Participants may listen to the audio via their computer speakers or headset, but presenters must dial in using the toll-free number to be heard. The presenter must speak into a telephone handset for the presentation, not a speaker phone. The volume and quality is affected with speaker phone usage. It is also recommended that both the participants and the presenter/producer close other applications to dedicate resources to the webinar. Table 7.2 compares features of the two systems.

Table 7.2. Feature Comparison of Blackboard and WebEx

BLACKBOARD	WEBEX
Embedded video, audio, data sharing	Embedded video, audio, data sharing
Evaluation tool for online assessments, interactive rubrics	Depends on type of WebEx
Social networking—blogs, discussion, group projects, wikis	Social networking
Active collaboration with breakout rooms, whiteboard, chat	Breakout rooms, whiteboard, chat
Management of multiple courses	
Customize to school/courses	
Recorded sessions	Recorded sessions
VOIP (audio from your computer) or phone access for audio	VOIP or phone access for audio

Note. VOIP = voice-over Internet protocol.

Figure 7.3. WebEx home page.

Moodle

Modular Object-Oriented Dynamic Learning Environment, or Moodle (http://moodle. org), is one of the world's largest and most widely used LMSs. It is also an open-source LMS, which means that anyone can run the system free of charge and modify it to create a more customized platform for delivering instruction. Demo sites are available to check out Moodle before signing up.

Adobe Acrobat Connect Pro

Connect Pro is an easy-to-use web-conferencing platform for web meetings, e-learning, and webinars. Because the Adobe Acrobat Connect virtual classroom needs only the free Adobe Flash Player to run, almost anyone can access the virtual classroom instantly, without having to download a special application or player before entering the virtual classroom. ConnectPro offers an intuitive interface and interactive tools. Educators and students can use any computer that supports the Adobe Flash Player on essentially any operating system, including Windows XP or Vista, Macintosh OS X, and Linux. Adobe Acrobat Connect Pro virtual classrooms can be managed directly from the user's web-based account through any browser on any platform. Blackboard and Moodle users can now access and manage Adobe Acrobat Connect Pro meetings directly from their environments.

Tegrity

Tegrity, a unit of McGraw-Hill Education, is a flexible software tool that can capture audio, video, and computer screen activity into a single "Tegrity session," which is automatically uploaded and then can be linked into a course. It is used by a number of universities, including Georgia Regents, University of Missouri at Kansas City, and University of Washington at Bothell. Tegrity can be used from Tegrity-enabled classrooms and from office or home computers to create lessons, demonstrations, critiques, podcasts, and other materials that can be accessed online.

Tips for the Instructor

For most effective use, consider the following tips as you get started:

- Join a few minutes early before your session to allow time for your system, such as WebEx or Blackboard, to download in your browser. On the day of your presentation, join thirty minutes before the event to set up and allow for troubleshooting.
- Dial in using the toll-free number, event number, and attendee number, which will pop up on the screen. If you do not see the instructions, go to the Info tab for help.
- When it is your turn to present, the facilitator will promote you from panelist to presenter, and you will be able to advance your own slides.
- Have an assistant moderate the chat and provide Q&A for your session.
- Become familiar with contact information and help for the system before your session.

Preparing to Teach Virtual Sessions

With the rapid increase in the number of distance students, coupled with the growing number of traditional students seeking information online, academic librarians are faced with the challenge of teaching information literacy to students who may never walk into the physical library.

Many higher education institutions include an information literacy class as a required part of the curriculum, often during a student's first year. The class may be offered as a separate class for credit or integrated into a survey course such as first-year English. These classes allow concepts to be covered in more depth than the one-shot class that librarians are often asked by faculty to give.

Information literacy courses have gained popularity because they offer opportunities for in-depth instruction and reinforcement of research skills through course activities. According to Jacobson and Mark (2000), this instruction is most effective when offered in context with content-based courses and assignments. Academic libraries have incorporated meaningful learning experiences into information literacy courses in a variety of ways:

- The University of Oregon's LIB 101 course uses a scenario-based approach by building assignments around research situations familiar to undergraduate students.
- Instructors of information literacy at the State University of New York College of Environmental Science and Forestry offer research assignments allowing students to address topics from their other courses.
- Montana State University College of Technology's information literacy course requires students to investigate a personal problem using information gathered throughout the course (Kaip, 2001).
- The University of Maryland offers a required online course, Information Literacy and Research Methods, in which students research a particular topic and participate in electronic discussions on timely research issues (Read, 2002).

Different subjects lend themselves to online instruction. The following lesson plans focus on online training in the form of webinars and blended instruction. Although the course topic and goals may be the same as a face-to-face course, the course layout, pacing, content delivery, and assignments will all be tailored for synchronous delivery, such as webinars where learners interact with one another and their instructors in real time—a virtual classroom. Although this is somewhat similar to classroom learning, the participants are separated by space or distance.

Introductory Online Lesson

An introductory lesson should get the online course off to a start that motivates students, forms a community, and allows attendees the opportunity to learn about the LMS or online tools that they will be using throughout the course. Issues surrounding copyright, the topic for this beginning lesson plan, is an important research subject. It can be taught totally online or through a blended approach, with part of the class online and part in person or some sessions online and some sessions face-to-face.

Step 1: Select an Activity

Icebreakers are a good introductory activity during which students can meet one another online and work together. In an icebreaker, an activity is given to the students that helps guide them to disclose information and thus create a comfortable learning environment. Such an activity helps set the tone for the course or unit of study. It also provides students with a fun way to learn how to use the LMS that will enable them to participate in the course.

Before logging on to the LMS, the instructor will provide directions for the activity in an online location linked to an initial welcome message. The instructions will include readings about the LMS so that students are familiar with many of its features that will be used during the course.

Step 2: Write Goal and Objectives

Plan the course by writing a general goal (or goals) and specific objectives for the entire course. The following are just for the introductory lesson.

Goal

After completing this lesson, students will have a general knowledge of the LMS, feel less isolated in the distance education environment, and begin to think about issues surrounding copyright.

Objectives

By the end of this lesson, students will be able to

- Use the class LMS features
- Differentiate among issues about copyright
- Recognize legal and illegal use of copyright
- Interact with other students in the online class

Step 3: Preplanning Your Course

As mentioned, preplanning an online course or material is vital to creating an effective end product. Becoming familiar with the LMS that will host your course comes first to learn about all the tools available as you work next on the content. Several short videos on the LMS website that you are using may help. For example, on Blackboard, you can find videos to get you started by viewing the Blackboard teaching series at http://www.youtube.com/playlist?list=PLontYaReEU1uoeMMSjknbmpd1TFFLWcRK. This collection of videos covers setting up your course, organizing content, motivating students, and much more. Next, become acquainted with the LMS tools, such as journals, discussion boards, surveys, assignments, and wikis, so that you can use them effectively with your students.

Step 4: Begin the Learning Activities

In this orientation activity, the instructor provides students with the opportunity to display prior knowledge on copyright by identifying correct and incorrect uses of web materials and have fun getting to know other students as they work together. As the instructor, you will also be able to isolate and identify student misconceptions about copyright, which you can then address during the course.

Activity 1: Identify and Use the Blackboard LMS Features

This activity is designed to acclimate students to the Blackboard LMS. Several tasks will demonstrate what they need to know to get started. Have students do the following.

1. Review the video for Global Navigation at https://help.blackboard.com/Special: Search?search=global navigation&path=en-us/Learn/*. Also, take a look at My Calendar and My Profile. You may want your students to set up a personal profile.
2. Review the course (or courses) they are enrolled in. Click the course title.
3. Review the parts of the course: announcements/alerts, getting started, syllabus, course modules, and other parts. Check for messages from their instructor, as well as grades as the course progresses. Continue to peruse the site.
4. Answer the following questions:
    a. How has the instructor organized the learning material on the LMS—learning modules, chapters, or another way?
    b. How is the navigation set up for your course (e.g., links at the top of the screen)?
    c. How do you get to Help? Discussion forums? Blackboard tools?
5. Play the video from Connecticut Community Colleges at http://www.youtube.com/watch?v=Y0tsujo8W9Y to view the different parts of Blackboard Learn designed for students, including tips such as turning off pop-up blockers, checking to make sure your e-mail address is correct, and setting preferences for notifications.
6. Review the Blackboard orientation course in which they are automatically enrolled.

Activity 2: Identify Copyright Violations and Legal Uses

Now that students are familiar with Blackboard Learn or their LMS, have them start the following activity about copyright. It will help you clarify for your class the concept of copyright—what is legal and what is a copyright violation. Your students will be working in groups of three. Make sure that you know in advance how to assign students to groups and what tools are available so they can collaborate. For Blackboard, review the video on creating groups at http://www.blackboard.com/quicktutorials/Bb9_Groups_Create_Groups_Add_Students.htm and http://ondemand.blackboard.com/communicate.htm. Have students complete the following tasks in groups of three:

1. Assign groups of three each on your LMS. You want them to review a website; some are listed here. Use http://blog.lib.umn.edu/copyinfo/scenarios/cat_all.html for copyright examples and http://www.thecopyrightsite.org/scenarios/deeplinking.html for copyright scenarios. Have them identify what they think is at least one copyright violation or one that is a legal use and why. They can make their comments on one of the tools (e.g., blog, wiki, journal). Have students in the group write their comments on their group page on whether they agree or disagree, and have them reach a consensus. Select a group leader to explain the group's reasoning to the rest of the class.
2. In the online forum, have them post in the chat the URLs of sites and why they feel they are copyright violations.

3. Show at least two websites online, and review the sites indicating why or why not there may be copyright violations.
4. Have each leader point out copyright violations for the group's website and explain why it is a violation or not. The rest of the class should agree or disagree in the chat and explain its reasoning.

Step 5: Evaluate What Was Learned

Ask students the following questions:

- How did you like this activity?
- After this activity, are you able to use the online tools that you will be using during the rest of the course?
- Do you understand what does and does not constitute copyright violation? What did you learn about copyright and plagiarism?

Adapt the rubric in table 7.3 to fit the activities in this lesson.

E-Learning Strategies

Performing this activity in a synchronous session to start off the course can help students' relax and can provide them with the opportunity to get used to the LMS during a low-stress activity. Troubleshooting technical difficulties are less stressful during a fun task, where time is not an issue and students can help one another.

- Linking an icebreaker activity to the actual content is a good way to meet two objectives with one activity.
- Make sure that you provide adequate feedback on this activity so that students will maintain their motivation to actively reflect on their learning.
- To motivate students and start the course on a positive note, provide a modest number of points toward the course grade through this activity.
- Come back to this activity later in the course, providing students the opportunity to reflect on what they learned and to reevaluate prior decisions on copyright.

Virtual Lesson Plan for Special Libraries

Face-to-face presentations about the information and data resources available to employees can be extremely valuable, but these opportunities are not always available to information professionals, and they do not address the continuing need to inform potential users about the new tools and services available to them. To communicate new information, information professionals need to take advantage of their organizations' existing communication channels or, using Web 2.0 and social networking tools, create their own. In many cases, because of their expertise in using these tools, information professionals have become their organizations' leaders in using social networks to achieve business objectives.

While many utilize vendor-developed training in the use of software and databases, a number of information professionals add specific examples that are highly relevant to their colleagues, such as detailed searches on the subjects of greatest interest to them and

Table 7.3. Rubric for Evaluating Online Courses

ADEQUATE	EFFECTIVE	EXEMPLARY
Students are uncertain about what is expected of them in the online environment.	Students can understand the key components and structure of the course; the course is organized and easy to follow.	Students can clearly understand all components and structure of the course; the course is well organized and easy to follow.
The aesthetic design (look) is rudimentary in conceptualization and construction.	The aesthetic design presents and communicates course information.	The aesthetic design effectively presents and communicates course information.
Web page structure and format are inconsistent.	There is consistency in some aspects of the web course.	There is consistency in all aspects of the web course.
Accessibility issues are not addressed.	Accessibility issues are somewhat addressed and comply with guidelines.	Accessibility issues are addressed.
Opportunities for student input and feedback are limited and inconsistent.	Opportunities exist for student input and feedback regarding course design and navigability.	Multiple opportunities for student input and feedback are integrated throughout the course.
Opportunities for interaction and communication limited.	Some opportunities for interaction and communication among students, between students and instructor, and between students and content.	Multiple opportunities for interaction and communication among students, between students and instructor, and between students and content.
Learning objectives are vague and may be incomplete. Performance expectations are unclear or absent.	Learning objectives are identified and performance expectations are implied.	Learning objectives and performance expectations are clearly defined.
Multiple learning styles are not recognized, accommodated, or integrated in the design of the course.	Strategies for meeting multiple learning styles are recognized, and attempts are made to ensure student understanding of content.	Strategies for meeting multiple learning styles and promoting critical thinking skills are clearly implemented.
Opportunities for student input and feedback about instructional design are limited and inconsistent.	Student feedback about instructional design is regularly collected.	Student feedback is regularly integrated into the instructional design and is used to inform decisions about instructional strategies.
Some of course objectives, instructional strategies, and assessment techniques may be aligned.	The course provides students the opportunity to self-assess their readiness for the online components/course.	The course requires students to self-assess their readiness for the online components/course prior to or at the beginning of the class.
Assessment strategies are not fully identified.	Course objectives, instructional strategies, and assessment techniques are somewhat aligned.	Course objectives, instructional strategies, and assessment techniques are closely aligned.
Assessment strategies are not comprehensive.	Assessment strategies are used to measure content knowledge, skills, and performance standards.	Ongoing multiple assessment strategies are used to measure content knowledge, skills, and performance standards.
Opportunities for students to receive feedback about their performance are infrequent and sporadic.	Opportunities for students to receive feedback about their performance are provided.	Students' self-assessment and/or peer feedback opportunities exist. Regular feedback about student performance is provided in a timely manner.

Table 7.3. Rubric for Evaluating Online Courses (*continued*)

ADEQUATE	EFFECTIVE	EXEMPLARY
Course uses a few technology tools for communication and learning.	Course uses some technology tools to facilitate communication and learning.	Course uses a variety of technology tools that are appropriate and effective for facilitating communication and learning.
Some technology may be used for its own sake.	Technology is mostly used to support student learning rather than for its own sake.	Technology is used to enhance student learning rather than for its own sake.
Multimedia and learning objects are largely absent.	Multimedia elements and/or learning objects may be used to engage students in the learning process.	Multimedia elements and/or learning objects are relevant, optimized for student Internet users, and effectively engage students in the learning process.
Opportunities for student feedback are limited.	Student feedback is used to assess delivery of course content.	Student feedback is used to continually improve technological delivery of course content.

their business. Many librarians also develop their own customized, downloadable, written materials.

The following lesson plan for a webinar takes into account the main subject orientation of a large biotech firm, where the library resides at the headquarters location but where training is needed at sites worldwide. The company now wants its scientists to do much of their own searching.

The module contains a series of online class sessions and exercises to teach question analysis, source selection, and search strategy development. ProQuest Dialog—a new, easy-to-use search system from Dialog—will be used. More than 100 databases in pharma/biomed, scitech, patents, and news/trade are accessible with varying levels of expertise needed to search the system, from novice to skilled to expert command searchers. The novice level will allow those scientists at the biotech company to do their own searches. More complicated searches may be done by the instruction librarian.

Step 1: Write General Goals and Specific Objectives

By working on different search systems, research scientists will become more familiar with databases in their company library that are accessible online.

Goals

At the end of these modules, searchers will be able to

- Conduct research in online databases on different search systems
- Work together in small and whole groups
- Participate in an online learning environment

Objectives

Researchers will be able to

- Create search strategies for bibliographic and full-text databases
- Analyze search strategies and revise them based on their analysis
- Conduct basic searches in ProQuest Dialog
- Find and use search aids to understand three search systems

Step 2: Gather Materials

The instruction librarian will have scientists use a search worksheet (figure 7.4) to write questions that they want to answer and to create their search strategies. To familiarize attendees with other search systems, the librarian will either create materials for Factiva, Thomson Reuters, and more or review them on the company's websites.

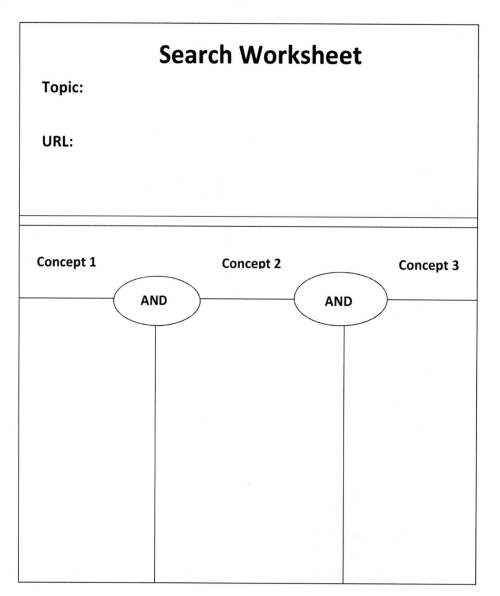

Figure 7.4. Search worksheet.

Step 3: Create Sample Activities

Depending on the patrons' level of search expertise and their knowledge of different search systems, the following activities encompass the entire search process and take three sessions to complete.

Activities to Introduce the Lessons

Before the first lesson, the instruction librarian will e-mail attendees materials on using WebEx and ProQuest Dialog, including a link to *A Getting Started Guide* at http://us.meetings.gsg.6.12.pdf, providing a quick look at functions of WebEx, as well as a quick tour at http://www.webex.com/products/elearning-and-online-training.html, which demonstrates some of the features of different WebEx systems. When attendees log onto WebEx for the first session, they should be familiar with the mechanics of the WebEx system. Attendees will also be instructed to bring sample problems that they want to research in each session based on the research they are working on.

Activities to Use during Lesson 1

In lesson 1, researchers will complete the following activities, working in pairs to create search questions and search strategies on ProQuest Dialog. The instruction librarian will do the following:

Activity 1: Provide information about the ProQuest Dialog search system, including databases offered that might be of interest to the group and a brief overview of the search system.

Activity 2: Write search questions on the whiteboard that have been brought into the library. These will provide models of appropriate search questions for attendees. Additional questions can be posed in the chat.

Activity 3: Provide one search term based on the search question and write it on the search worksheet. Then ask attendees to write additional search terms in the chat. Discussion of terms takes place. The instructor can poll attendees to determine which terms they think are the best for the search.

Activity 4: Explain the need for synonyms for the main search terms, and ask for more terms in the chat.

Activity 5: Ask attendees to explain and illustrate Boolean connectors (e.g., AND, OR, NOT).

Activity 6: Ask groups of three, using the breakout WebEx feature, to create a search question and complete a search worksheet using figure 7.4, including search terms, synonyms, and Boolean connectors.

Activity 7: Select each group to present its search worksheet, justifying the terms and synonyms it chose. Other group members comment in the chat on each group's search.

The instruction librarian offers comments on the search strategies, answers questions, and gives assignments for the following class.

Assignment 1: Attendees will create at least three of their own search strategies to be discussed in the next session and complete three from the class handout of problem questions. Attendees are expected to have completed the exercises and to be prepared to discuss search strategies and results at the next session. They will e-mail their assignments to the instructor the day before the following session. A model search for each exercise will be posted before the next class and will include general comments to the entire class on problems noted and provide suggestions for improving search performance.

Assignment 2: Using links to materials on the ProQuest Dialog website at http://www.dialog.com/products/ under the Content and Databases tab, attendees will review the categories and descriptions of the databases and select one or two databases that they think they would use for their searches.

Assignment 3: Attendees will review YouTube videos showing how to conduct a basic search in ProQuest Dialog at http://support.dialog.com/training/proquestdialog/#tabview=tab2. Both videos have exercises to reinforce what participants learned about a basic search on ProQuest Dialog.

Activities to Use during Lesson 2

In lesson 2, researchers will again work in groups of three to review search questions and strategies that they plan to conduct on ProQuest Dialog. For the next activities, the instructor will do the following:

- *Activity 1*: Provide each group with several unnamed strategies so that group members do not review their own strategies. In breakout rooms, groups will each select a leader and then analyze the strategies, providing comments and suggestions. The leader will present one strategy that the group thinks is good and one that needs changing, as well as the reasons for his or her judgment, to the entire group. Other attendees can respond and ask questions using the chat.
- *Activity 2*: Introduce ProQuest Dialog, and conduct one of the group searches in selected databases to illustrate how to conduct a search in ProQuest Dialog. Having seen the video, attendees should be somewhat familiar with the search process. Use the chat for questions and comments.
- *Activity 3*: Have each group appoint a presenter to demonstrate a search on ProQuest Dialog to show on WebEx. Discussion and Q&A in the chat will follow.
- *Activity 4*: Using the hands-on lab feature, have groups work on remote PCs to run additional searches based on the strategies they received (e.g., select databases, enter search strategies, review and analyze results for relevance, review other search options such as "limit by date").
- *Activity 5*: Have each group select one search to run for the entire group. They should select a presenter who has not conducted a live search before the entire group. Discussion and analysis on the searches follow.

The instructor provides additional assignments before the next session.

- *Assignment 1:* Attendees will review the advanced search ProQuest Dialog YouTube video at http://support.dialog.com/training/proquestdialog/#tabview=tab2. Attendees in the same location may work together in pairs to prepare one question analysis worksheet, describe the intended approach, perform and save the search, review and critique the search, and prepare questions for clarification.

- *Assignment 2:* Student pairs are encouraged to submit *one* annotated search via e-mail after each session. For submission, students may select a search that they were unable to resolve or one that they feel was a good example.
- *Assignment 3*: Attendees will be given their portfolio assignment and should start on this before the final session. See evaluation for details about the portfolio.

Activities to Use during Lesson 3

Attendees will use techniques similar to those in lesson 2 to review their assignment and practice searching using the advanced search on ProQuest Dialog. The next assignment is to complete activities in follow-up to the lesson.

Activities as Follow-Up to the Lessons

- Select another search system (e.g., Factiva, EBSCO, ProQuest) and conduct searches using what you learned searching ProQuest Dialog.
- Create a chart demonstrating similarities and differences between the two systems.
- Evaluate the two systems (e.g., which was easier to use, which retrieved most relevant results, how did the content in both compare).
- Attendees will present their searches in their portfolios using various online tools, including the whiteboard, video, PowerPoint, and demonstrations of searches, to name some.

Step 4: Evaluate What Was Learned

Both formative and summative evaluation is part of assessment for these lessons.

Formative evaluation consists of the study of early searches. These searches will not be checked individually, but comments on them will clearly indicate the level of competence with the searches. A model search for each exercise will be posted online after each is due and will include general comments to the entire class on problems noted and provide suggestions for improving search performance.

Summative evaluation includes a search portfolio in three parts with annotated bibliographic and full-text searches.

Evaluation Rubric

Part 1: Bibliographic searching. This section contains bibliographic searches with strategies.

- Complete four questions with brief overview of the search strategy, the annotated search, and search critique (one double-spaced page for each search), as well as two searches each using basic and advanced search.
- Demonstrate competencies for search strategies. Thoughtful annotations show reaction to output, awareness of problems, and how and why the strategy is amended.

Well-written search critique includes discussion of what went wrong and right and how to improve the strategy and the search.

Part 2: Full-text searching. This section focuses on strategies for full-text searching and might include comparisons of searching different full-text databases or systems, techniques for finding images, and so on.

- Well-written discussion of full-text searching with examples (approximately three double-spaced pages), as described earlier.
- Conduct two searches using basic and advanced search in ProQuest Dialog.
- Create a chart of differences between basic and advanced search on ProQuest Dialog and identify the advantages and disadvantages of each.

Part 3: Another search system. Conduct two searches using another search system of your choice (e.g., ProQuest, Factiva, Thomson Reuters). Compile same information as before. Present the portfolio.

⊚ Key Points

As online instruction becomes even more commonplace, teaching webinars, participating in a blended learning environment, and coteaching or facilitating online instruction will become an integral and time-consuming task of instruction librarians. In fact, more librarians will be called on to conduct formalized instruction than ever before.

Technology continues to become more sophisticated, and the need for online learning continues to grow. This chapter provides keys to get started, lessons to use as models, and sites to visit to learn more. See table 7.4 for more resources.

Think about the following as you enter online instruction.

- Provide a means of social learning when the learners are spaced apart. This learning is important for
  - solving small everyday problems before they get big
  - creating an environment that supports creativity
  - forming ad hoc workgroups as needed to address business challenges
  - building a work environment that is flexible.
- Guide patrons to create their own collaborative knowledge bases, rather than have them rely on others to do it for them.
- Increase the feeling of being a team when the learners are separated by distance by increasing participation and developing community.
- Help motivate participants in your sessions as this is a primary requirement for learning.

EXERCISES: Now You Try It . . .

1. To find out more about basic computer, Internet, e-mail, and study skills, try this Learn to Learn tutorial at http://www.waol.org/learnToLearn/Module1/mod1_01.htm.

Table 7.4. URLs for Chapter 7

DESCRIPTION	URL
Virginia Commonwealth pilot online library training	http://www.sla.org/pdfs/sla2007/kirlewonlinelibinstrsvcs.pdf
Small public library program to instruct job hunters on computer basics	http://www.webjunction.org/resources/WebJunction/Documents/webjunction/Project%20Compass%20Workbook_04.12.pdf
Videos on topics such as computer basic skills	http://pascolibraries.org/egovtools.shtml
Workforce services	http://www.webjunction.org/explore-topics/workforce-resources/materials.html
Website with examples of embedded librarians	http://embeddedlibrarian.com
How-to videos for tech basics, Internet, communication, media	http://www.teachparentstech.org/watch
ADDIE video	http://www.youtube.com/watch?v=jiLLz1SaxGc
How-to videos on using Blackboard	http://ondemand.blackboard.com/understand.htm
Blackboard 9.1 for beginners	http://www.youtube.com/watch?v=S54vkmSIpBY
Blackboard 9.1 for students	http://www.youtube.com/watch?v=Y0tsujo8W9Y
Moodle demo sites	http://demo.moodle.net http://school.demo.moodle.net
Blackboard series of webinars or recordings for instructors	http://www.youtube.com/watch?v=Loz2TXgw4tA&list=PLontYaReEU1uoeMMSjknbmpd1TFFLWcRK&index=1
Differences between Blackboard and Moodle	http://www.youtube.com/watch?v=B6-Rf7yAoeU
Moodle in the classroom	http://www.youtube.com/watch?v=Z9XfwBzt1mY&list=PL48100C65B48DFC48

Note. ADDIE = analysis, design, development, implementation, evaluation.

2. Watch the video at http://www.youtube.com/watch?v=fFOT5De1o58 and answer the following questions:
   - How would you describe the video instructor's class to an outsider?
   - What kind of instructional strategies did you observe?
   - Do you agree with the strategies used? Please explain.
   - Did you feel that learning took place—if so, to what extent?
   - How much of yourself do you see in the instructor and why?
   - What would you add or do differently in the scenario?
3. Complete a single pilot implementation of one web-based instruction program for a targeted segment of public library patrons (e.g., teens, senior citizens, unemployed). Evaluate and document the outcomes of this planning project.

⊚ References

Jacobson, Trudi E., and Beth L. Mark. 2000. "Separating Wheat from Chaff: Helping First Year Students Become Information Savvy." *Journal of General Education* 49 (4): 256–78.

Kaip, S. 2001. "It's Not Just for Term Papers: Solving Real-Life Problems in an Information Literacy Course." *College and Research Libraries News* 62 (5): 496–98.

Read, B. 2002. "An Online Course Teaches Students to Use Libraries and the Internet—and Avoid Plagiarism." *Chronicle of Higher Education*, May 17. http://lists.cas.usf.edu/pipermail/chemfaculty/2002-May/002115.html.

⊚ Further Reading

Becker, S., M. D. Crandall, K. E. Fisher, B. Kinney, C. Landry, and A. Rocha. 2010. *Opportunity for All: How the American Public Benefits from Internet Access at U.S. Libraries.* Washington, DC: Institute of Museum and Library Services.

Bertot, J. C., A. McDermott, R. Lincoln, B. Real, and K. Peterson. 2012. *2011–2012 Public Library Funding and Technology Access Survey: Survey Findings and Report.* College Park, MD: University of Maryland College Park, Information Policy and Access Center. http://www.plinternetsurvey.org.

Bullmaster-Day, Marcella. 2011. "Online and Blended Learning: What the Research Says." White paper. New York: Kaplan K12 Learning Services.

Dziuban, Charles D., Joel L. Hartman, and Patsy D. Miskual. 2004. "Blended Learning." *Research Bulletin* 7 (March 30). University of Central Florida, Center for Applied Research. http://net.educause.edu/ir/library/pdf/erb0407.pdf.

Elkins, E., J. A. Ellis, Verostek, and J. Williamson. 2001. "ESF 200, Information Literacy: Syllabus and Workforms." State University of New York College of Environmental Science and Forestry, Moon Library.

Fabry, D. L. 2009. "Designing Online and On-Ground Courses to Ensure Comparability and Consistency in Meeting Learning Outcomes." *Quarterly Review of Distance Education* 10 (3): 253–61.

Frantz, P. 2002. "A Scenario-Based Approach to Credit Course Instruction." *Reference Services Review* 30 (1): 37–42.

Jacobson, Trudi E., and Laura B. Cohen. 2002. "Evaluating Internet Sites: The Challenge Continues." *Teaching Professor* 16 (7): 2.

Kobzina, N. G. 2010. "A Faculty–Librarian Partnership: A Unique Opportunity for Course Integration." *Journal of Library Administration* 50 (4): 293–314.

Mackey, Thomas P., and Trudi E. Jacobson. 2005. "Information Literacy: A Collaborative Endeavor." *College Teaching* 53 (4): 140–44.

———, eds. 2011. *Teaching Information Literacy Online.* New York: Neal-Schuman.

Staker, H. 2011. *The Rise of K–12 Blended Learning: Profiles of Emerging Models.* Mountain View, CA: Innosight Institute.

Varvel, V. E., Jr. 2002. "Ice-Breakers." *Pointer and Clickers: ION's Technology Tip of the Month* 4 (1). http://www.ion.uillinois.edu/resources/pointersclickers/2002_01/index.asp.

Asynchronous Instruction

SELF-DIRECTED, or asynchronous, instruction is learning initiated and directed by the learner and can include self-paced, independent, and individualized learning as well as self-instruction. Whatever terminology is used, self-directed learning places the responsibility for learning directly on the learner. The independent learner is one who is more involved and active within the learning process. Online learning supports the self-directed learner in pursuing individualized, self-paced instructional activities.

This chapter covers diverse self-paced materials, from individualized tutorials to online materials and print search aids. You will see how academic, special, and public libraries are using self-directed materials, and you will look in-depth at videos, Pinterest, and LibGuides. Finally, two model lessons will help you as you prepare your self-paced materials for your library.

Tutorials work well when introducing new concepts, reviewing difficult ideas, or providing enrichment. For example, public libraries use self-paced materials to teach life skills such as resume writing or basic technology.

Libraries are creating a myriad of self-directed materials to teach their patrons—from subject guides to videos or screencasts to LibGuides to tutorials. The examples that follow illustrate some of these created and used by public, academic, and special libraries. Several of these materials are described in detail in this chapter.

Example 1: Academic Guides

Subject or course guides identify useful library and web resources pertinent to researchers in a specific discipline or department. These guides provide a broad overview of resources in a given subject area. Course guides are one-stop webpages that assist students with their research. They include descriptions of relevant print and electronic resources, links, and lists of the most important reference sources. In addition, they provide research strategies, tips for evaluating information sources, and links to appropriate citation guides. Faculty and subject librarians at the University of Missouri (http://mulibraries.missouri.edu/guides/classestours/instructionplan.htm#tabs-4) work together to create customized webpages for their classes and assignments. Faculty often link to subject guides from courseware or course webpages.

Example 2: Academic Tutorials

Web tutorials are a great way of providing information literacy training. These tutorials are a good fit for distance students because they can be accessed at any time and can allow students to work at their own pace. Another benefit of the web tutorial is that, unlike in-class instruction, the web tutorial can be revisited to reiterate information literacy skills to students. Due to the self-paced nature of the web tutorial, more information literacy skills can be addressed; for instance, skills such as Boolean operators can be looked at in-depth, whereas in a classroom setting, there may not be enough time. Patrons also have the ability to skip ahead in a tutorial if it covers information they already know. It further allows the student to spend more time in areas of difficulty. This degree of self-pacing is not available during in-class instruction.

A common type of web-based library tutorial deals with general research or reference skills, which can be integrated into academic courses, meet the needs of special libraries in different disciplines, and work well for those who do not have the opportunity to receive face-to-face training or for those who need to refresh their skills. Typical topics include planning research, identifying and refining a topic, using research tools, evaluating information, and differentiating among types of resources.

The California State University Information Competence Project presents information literacy instruction tutorials in a visually interesting environment and addresses mass media literacy. Interactive learning exercises and diverse audiovisual components (e.g., sound, QuickTime movies, animations) are incorporated.

The University of Washington Information Literacy Learning initiative, or "UWill," is designed to teach information literacy skills in context with course objectives. Customized tutorials assist students in completing course assignments while developing information competencies.

Other instruction librarians are using the "flipped classroom" concept as part of blended instruction. For example, before the online class session, the instructor can have students review information skills tutorials about online databases on a search system or creating search strategies. The advantage of such tools is that it leaves more class time for discussion and questions. With the combination of video and audio, the expert can mimic the one-on-one experience and deliver clear, complete instructions. From the learner's point of view, this instruction provides the ability to pause and repeat the instruction; it gives learners the advantage of moving at their own paces, something that a classroom session cannot always offer. For example, such tutorials at MedlinePlus (http://www.nlm.nih.gov/medlineplus/tutorials/) provide information on many health topics that would be useful for patrons at a public library to review.

Example 3: Technology

In some cases, librarians leverage their tech savvy to raise their profiles on campus beyond the scope of research—for instance, by assisting faculty in creating websites or media. Bailey, Blunt, and Magner (2011) describe how librarians leveraged technology skills—in this case, video and multimedia creation—to support faculty goals, instruction, and conference presentations. This emphasizes the importance of librarians on campus and may build a foundation for greater partnerships. In addition to video creation, it is common for librarians to work with faculty in groups or one-on-one to assist with new technologies such as blogs, mobile access, social media, and RSS.

Example 4: Online Search Aids

Along with having videos, the University of Hawaii library has resources in other categories:

- Interactive websites where the user can input information on his or her topic and get something useful back
- Content web information, usually "static" pages with useful text
- Handouts—information in paper format or PDF that addresses a particular activity (e.g., MLA citations)

Example 5: Screencasts and Videos

A recent tool in the e-learning sector is screencasting. A screencast is a digital recording of computer screen output, also known as a video screen capture, often containing audio narration. A screencast is essentially a movie of the changes over time that a user sees on a computer screen, enhanced with audio narration.

The University of Hawaii, for example, has videos explaining concepts, processes, and other activities connected to college research papers and projects. The Lilo Tutorial at http://www.hawaii.edu/lilo/fall12/info/faculty/resources_quickview.php is a good self-paced example. It combines a tutorial with videos to explain how to conduct professional research skills. The tutorial moves step-by-step through the stages of completing a research project, from beginning through organizing, searching, and evaluating the work.

Videos throughout provide questions, as well as a calendar to create. Subtopics cover details on all steps in the process.

Numerous tutorials, with and without audio, are available at http://www.clipinfolit. org/tutorials. These are offered through a Creative Commons license and will serve as excellent models for your tutorials in any type of library. These screencasts were created with Adobe Captivate (see table 8.1).

Table 8.1. Tutorials/Screencasts

DESCRIPTION	URL
Developing a topic	http://www.wou.edu/provost/library/clip/tutorials/dev_topic.htm
Deconstructing a citation	http://www.clipinfolit.org/tutorials/deconstructing-citations
Generating search terms	http://www.clipinfolit.org/tutorials/generating-search-terms
What is a library database?	http://www.clipinfolit.org/tutorials/what-is-a-library-database
Why to cite sources?	http://www.clipinfolit.org/tutorials/why-you-need-to-cite-sources
Evaluating Internet sources	http://www.clipinfolit.org/tutorials/evaluating-internet-resources

◎ Considerations When Using Video

The previous section provides examples of self-paced instruction. This section explains more fully the advantages and disadvantages of using video, as well as how to use it as a teaching tool and how to create it.

Advantages

While online videos offer benefits with efficiency and engagement, they cannot substitute for the rich interaction of in-person, classroom instruction. As with any teaching materials, however, video has its advantages and disadvantages. Although it may not measure up to face-to-face classroom instruction, video has its uses. The following comparison illustrates the benefits and disadvantages of video with classroom instruction.

Available on the popular YouTube website and searchable in Google, instructional videos allow you to demonstrate tasks, project steps, calculations, and anything that is easier to show rather than to describe. These videos are especially beneficial for instruction that needs visual elements, such as a simulation or demonstration. Numerous benefits include

- Potential responsiveness to learning needs, due to individual control of the pace and timing
- Suitability for different learning styles (e.g., listen to a minilecture, watch a demonstration, read a summary; review learning styles in chapter 2)
- Quick viewing, with most videos designed at five minutes or less
- Capability of addressing a single research problem or skill
- Review lessons with video summaries

- Greater reach to patrons locally and globally
- Higher initial costs but lower ongoing time commitment and financial costs
- Fewer geographic and scheduling constraints
- Compatible with iPhone and other mobile devices, a television, or a computer
- May meet patrons' technology expectations and need for timely assistance
- Reuse through placement of videos on library website
- Potential to embed in other instructional material
- Content evaluation possible

Disadvantages

Despite the number of advantages, it is still important to make sure that disadvantages will not be too much of a challenge to prepare and deliver the instruction for your library. Disadvantages to video include

- Needing a person with instructional design skills and knowledge of video software package
- Requiring more time for initial preparation
- Having less interaction with end users, with no real-time activity tailored to learning needs
- Potentially not forging a personal connection with patrons
- Creating fewer opportunities to assess students' learning and respond to their questions

Video as a Teaching Tool

Video is now incredibly easy to create, manipulate, and make available online. Videos can even be captured with a cell phone or basic digital camera. They can be created with free downloadable software, such as Jing, or more sophisticated packages, such as Camtasia or Captivate. For example, the Chemistry and Chemical Engineering Library at the University of California, Berkeley, created online instructional videos for PubChem (http://pubchem.ncbi.nlm.nih.gov), a free database of the biological activities of small molecules, developed by the National Center for Biotechnology Information at the National Institutes of Health. The videos are modular, with each one addressing research problems and tasks in chemical informatics. The videos were created to showcase the library and facilitate patron use. The videos are available anytime, anywhere, and they facilitate self-directed learning at a pace and environment suitable to different learning styles.

Preplanning the Video

Preplanning before actually producing the video is the most important and time-consuming part of creating a video. A storyboard is a graphic organizer that allows the librarian, often with the help of an instruction designer, to visualize and detail all aspects of the plan. All parts of the video are included—narration, images, titles, transitions, special effects, music, and sounds. The storyboard lets the creators organize their thoughts before they begin on the computer. It also supplies a visual plan that others can review and revise so that everyone can see where new resources or directions are needed before beginning to write. The storyboard forms the roadmap for the video, indicating both time (what happens first, second, and third) and interaction—how the audio, voice-over narrative, and music interact with the images or video. It shows where and how visual effects, transitions, animations, and organization of the screen will be used.

The script is the main part of the message that you want to convey. Start with an outline that defines the main points to be made in the instruction. The script includes all aspects of the content: the wording for the text, media that illustrate the content (images, sound, movies, etc.), activities to reinforce a concept, and skill checks to provide an assessment of whether users have retained what has been taught.

Depending on the complexity of the video content, a storyboard can be as simple as a posterboard with sticky notes stuck on it; you can create one with Microsoft Word; or you can use a ready-made template, such as the following:

PowerProduction Software—http://www.powerproduction.com/license_management .html

Storyboard Quick Software—http://www.storyboardquick.com/product-info/

Featured Storyboard Pro Software—http://storyboard-pro.software.informer.com

Using Video Software

There is software to create video that fits any library's budget. Jing, created by TechSmith, is free, simple to use, and enables you to capture activity as you complete it on a computer screen. Two well-known professional packages are Camtasia Studio (TechSmith) and Captivate, created by Adobe, both at a cost with an educational price. You can record segments of an audio or video lecture to post online for patrons to view and add comments.

Captivate, at http://www.adobe.com/support/captivate/gettingstarted.html, lets you easily create product demonstrations in HD, application simulations, and compliance training. You can import PowerPoint slides and enrich instruction with multimedia, interactive elements, and quizzes. You can deliver content to virtually any device, including iPads. You can publish your projects to the Internet, desktops, YouTube, and leading SCORM- and AICC-compliant learning management systems to track student progress. SCORM is a technical standard that governs how online learning content and learning management systems communicate with each other. You can deliver HTML5-based content to mobile devices, including iPads. You can transform PowerPoint presentations into interactive e-learning content. The SCORM standard makes sure that all instructional material and learning management systems can work with each other.

Camtasia Studio and Camtasia for Mac, at http://www.techsmith.com/camtasia. html, are easy-to-use screen-capturing and editing software applications for creating video tutorials and presentations. TechSmith offers useful, well-designed video and PDF tutorials, starting with links provided while you download the program.

Jing (http://www.techsmith.com/jing.html) is a free screencasting computer program. Users must sign up for an account before using the software. It is often used by librarians to assist library users in finding information, answering questions, and fulfilling users' information needs. Jing is compatible with Macintoch and Microsoft Windows. Review table 8.2 to compare types of programs used in video production.

Table 8.2. Comparison of Types of Programs Used in Video Production

TOOL USED	FUNCTION	COST
Microsoft PowerPoint[a]	Create slide content	Available at many academic libraries. Can also use OpenOffice.org or Google Docs for free
GIMP[b]	Edit graphics	Free, open-source software
Audacity[c]	Record and edit audio	Free, open-source software for PC
Screencast-o-Matic[d]	Make screencasts (e.g., record computer demos with video and audio)	Free for the basic program
Windows Live Movie Maker[e]	Edit video	Free
YouTube[f]	Store and distribute videos	Free

[a]http://office.microsoft.com/en-us/powerpoint/.
[b]http://www.gimp.org.
[c]http://audacity.sourceforge.net/download/.
[d]http://www.screencast-o-matic.com.
[e]http://windows-live-movie-maker.en.softonic.com.
[f]http://www.youtube.com.

Beginning Production

Although the storyboard provides the initial decisions and elements, the production phase is the time to combine the elements in a compelling instructional video. Production contains two parts. The first draft provides the creator with a complete view of the video, which includes the sequencing of images, titles, and descriptions. It illustrates the flow of the instruction. This draft does not have audio, music, transitions, or special effects. Authors can review the draft, to make sure that nothing is missing, and have others also review it. The final product contains all parts—audio, music, transitions—that appeared in the storyboard. At this point, review should make sure that all elements lead toward improving the learning.

Publishing the Video

The video can be published to your library website or created as a stand-alone video. It can also be published as a YouTube video. YouTube dedicates an entire section of its site to educational offerings at http://www.youtube.com/education (see figure 8.1). At YouTube Education, instructors and organizations can create their own channels to share video content. You can find everything from university lectures to homemade how-to demos.

⑥ Online Search Aids

Over the years, libraries have created a number of types of printed search aids—quick reference cards, search guides, and library guides. Several new materials in all types of libraries are gaining popularity—LibGuides and Pinterest. Here we take a look at both.

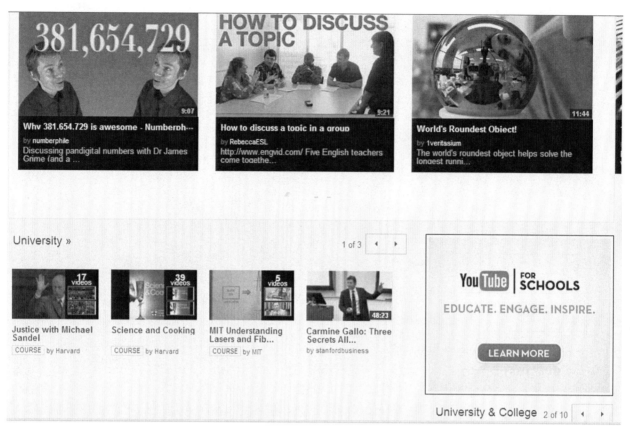

Figure 8.1. YouTube Education home page.

LibGuides

LibGuides are a Web 2.0 content management and publishing system that allow librarians to create subject research guides. Academic libraries create them to provide resources for classes; public libraries provide them to help patrons improve their information literacy. Special libraries use them to learn more about special databases provided by an organization.

The instruction librarian may use the LibGuide program to create subject guides or course guides of suggested resources or tutorials and strategies for researching specific assignments. Usually created in a tabbed structure, they can be divided by type of resource (e.g., articles, databases, videos) or aspects of a course (e.g., accounting, finance, marketing).

LibGuides can offer a variety of resources about a specific subject. For example, a special or academic library might offer ABI/INFORM, a database containing business and management content. An ABI/INFORM LibGuide, set up in a tabular design, might contain tabs to include content, publication coverage, search tips, searchable fields, and sample searches. Other tabs might cover information about live webinars and recordings, as well as screencasts illustrating how to use ABI on the ProQuest platform.

To create your own LibGuides, you do not have to start from scratch. Viewing LibGuides and reviewing guidelines from librarians who have already created them can be very useful.

LibGuide Models for Special, Academic, and Public Libraries

Although special software is needed to create LibGuides, they are found in many libraries—as simple as one page and as complex as multiple tabs containing text, video, photos, and more.

Example 1: LibGuides in Special Libraries

The LibGuides created by the Fred Hutchinson Cancer Research Center at http://libguides.fhcrc.org/browse.php offer LibGuides designed for graduate courses in cell migration or virology (see figure 8.2). LibGuides are available for academic courses such as Immunity, with tabs to course information, the course syllabus and readings, and study questions—all easily found in one location. A topic such as "electron microscopy resources and training" is an excellent model for a medical school special library or a biotech corporate library to use to create their own LibGuides.

Example 2: LibGuides in Public Libraries

In a tight economy, patrons have turned to their public libraries to help them learn skills such as writing a resume, participating in an interview, improving computer use, and more, to help them find a job or change careers. Contra Costa Public Library (http://guides.ccclib.org/jobs) created a LibGuide specifically to help these patrons. It offers many resources under the tabs Finding Jobs, Applying for Jobs, Filing for Unemployment, Internet and Computer Basics, and Local Job Training. This LibGuide handles an unemployed worker's needs all in one location.

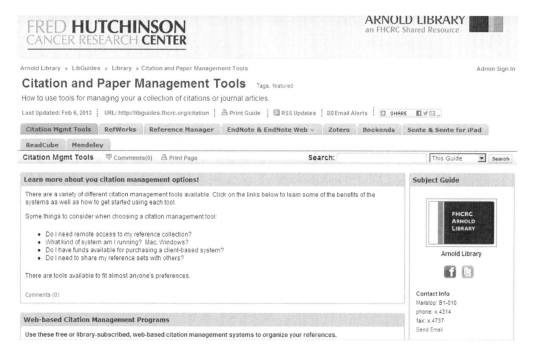

Figure 8.2.   Fred Hutchinson Cancer Research Center.

Example 3: LibGuides in Academic Libraries

Archer Library at the University of Regina (http://uregina.libguides.com/), has a wide store of LibGuides encompassing an alphabetical listing of subjects and librarians assigned to each subject. For example, specific courses have their own LibGuides, illustrating how to search for topics in a particular subject, such as anthropology. Several tabbed entries take the user through creating search strategies, using the library catalog, modifying a strategy, working with results, and even researching with e-books, a popular alternative today. Another LibGuide describes how to evaluate journal articles and websites. Guides are sorted by Featured, Popular, Recent, Contact Information, Ask an Expert, and more.

This comprehensive group of LibGuides even supplies a "Quickstart Help & Standards" guide (http://uregina.libguides.com/standards) to provide instructions on creating your own subject-specific or course LibGuide, including creating a profile, designing the guide, linking to materials, adding content and contact information, and publishing the guide. The Archer Library guide also contains sample topics covering how to cite sources, with tabs containing resources on RefWorks, a cited reference program, and different cited reference styles (e.g., MLA, APA, Chicago). See figure 8.3 to get started with the nuts and bolts of putting together your own library LibGuide.

Pinterest

Pinterest (http://pinterest.com) is a popular social media site with individual users, businesses, and nonprofits. It is a virtual pinboard to organize and publicize library resources by

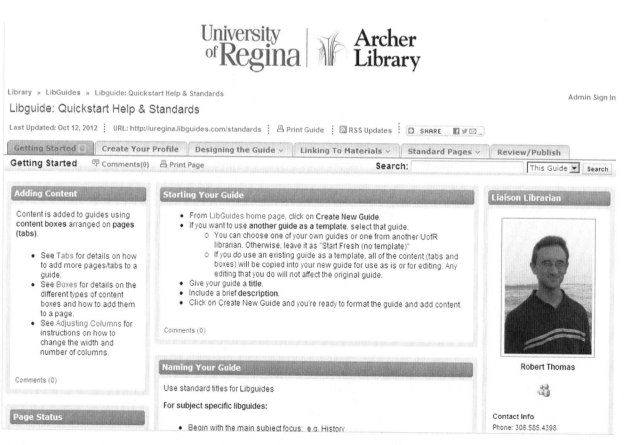

Figure 8.3. "Quickstart Help & Standards" guide.

"pinning" up images that you discover online or add yourself. Begun in 2011, Pinterest has quickly become one of the top-10 most trafficked social networking websites according to a marketing study by Experian Hitwise (2012). During the second week in December, the website had over eleven million visitors. It serves as a way to share pictures and infographics and visually curate online resources for your own use or collaboratively. You can create different boards for different topics or areas of interest. You can browse other people's boards, and they can browse yours to see what they find interesting, even on a mobile or tablet. Besides all the great programming ideas, Pinterest has a wealth of display ideas. Many are ideas from other libraries. Figure 8.4 gives the basics of using Pinterest.

While Pinterest a way to connect with your favorite authors, publishers, libraries, and people you know, it is also an easy way to find great craft ideas, recipes, and display ideas and to connect your library to your community.

When initiating a pinboard, consider who will pin and who has access, as well as credits and permissions. Elements needing attention include marketing, training staff, policies for content, and metrics to see who is viewing your board. Finally, certain skills should be taught. Librarians can assist researchers and students on how to apply Pinterest to their courses, and they can help patrons in public libraries use Pinterest effectively and ethically.

Pinterest is continuing to grow, but changes are expected, including more understanding of managing copyright and more content and resource sharing. Many of the handouts

Figure 8.4. Pinterest 101.

and guides so familiar to librarians will become more visual, especially with end users becoming Pinterest users.

Examples of Public Library Pinterests

Public libraries are using Pinterest as a way to share ideas and information about their services and resources with their patrons, market their sources, and encourage patrons to visit the library and participate in a variety of library programs. Public libraries also share information about their communities and use a board as a reference service, pinning answers to FAQs and commonly used reference sources. See figure 8.5 to learn from examples of other public libraries:

- Oakland Public Library's Teen Zone at http://pinterest.com/oplteenzone/ has a number of boards appealing to teens. One goal is to get young people to read by pinning teen picks and vampire books; other boards encourage teens to get involved in projects, partner with local artists, and volunteer their time. The visual representation of the Pinterest boards entices teens to participate.
- Columbus Metropolitan Library at http://lj.libraryjournal.com/2012/02/industry-news/use-pinterest-to-promote-your-programs-and-services/ uses Pinterest to pin book covers to showcase new books and children's books. It is a good way to visualize what you have in your collection. Other public libraries using Pinterest include New York Public Library–Westerville, Muncie Public Library, Fullerton Public Library, and more.
- San Francisco Public Library is showcasing historic images in the city's libraries of San Francisco Bay during World War II (http://www.cr.nps.gov/nr/travel/wwII bayarea/sitelist.htm).
- Sacramento Public Library (http://pinterest.com/saclib/) pins visual reading lists on a variety of subjects, from librarians' favorites to sports to kid-friendly books.
- Burlington Public Library (http://www.burlington.lib.wa.us) offers a diverse board with best reads, free instruction on computers, and questions important to patrons.

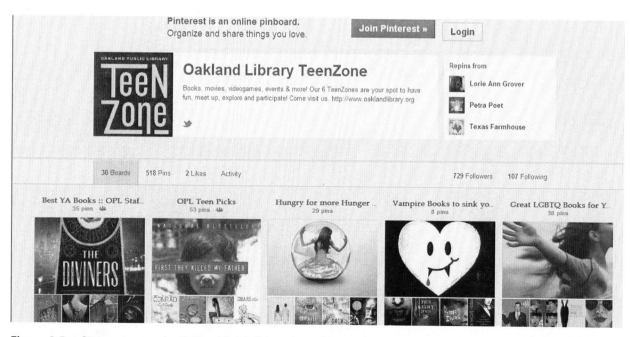

Figure 8.5. Pinterest example: Oakland Public Library's Teen Zone.

Examples of Academic and Research Library Pinterests

Pinterest is important for academic and research libraries because of its implications for information usage, content sharing, service enhancements, opportunities for collaboration, and potential as a marketing tool. The Association of College and Research Libraries at http://www.ala.org/acrl/pinterest is showing how academic libraries are using Pinterest as a valuable research tool, especially when it comes to tracking archival content such as images and documents. There are many uses:

- Curate instruction resources; show a resource discovery tool; illustrate proper citation and ethical use; and pin reference resources and diagrams to commonly asked questions.
- Pin instructional videos, interviews, and tutorials on your board.
- Use Pinterest for class projects, course assignments, or labs.
- Complement subject guides such as LibGuides or create visual bookmarking.
- Introduce the library and its services.
- Create a pinboard to complement online tutorials, supplement class handouts, and pin videos or screenshots of search techniques.

The Townsend Memorial Library at the University of Mary Hardin-Baylor has created a number of Pinterest boards. Their Research and Tips board contains versatile information on job interview questions, differences between scholarly and popular journals, Boolean logic, videos, information about social networking sites such as Facebook and Flickr, and uses of Creative Commons.

⑥ Other Materials

There are many other types of resources that instructor librarians might create for their patrons: PDF handouts (e.g., quick reference cards, how-to guides) and discussion boards, blogs, and wikis for announcements of events. For example, the Pima County Library has created a guide of eleven lessons to troubleshoot accessing the library catalog, the library databases, and a patron's library account. The simple step-by-step instructions at http://www.library.pima.gov/help/guide.php#spyware take the patron through each process.

In public, academic, and special academic libraries, library orientation tours are a beneficial way to guide new students and patrons through the departments, services, and materials located in the library. A virtual library tour can achieve the same purpose. It provides patrons with a map that they can use to become acquainted with the library building and its services. An informative video tour of the Syracuse University libraries at http://library.syr.edu/about/tour/ takes you through the six libraries, with a detailed tour of each floor of the main library, identifying each area, from reading rooms to the DVD/audio space to special collections. This is an excellent model for anyone looking to create a tour of their library (see figure 8.6).

Next, you will see two practical applications—how to create a video and a LibGuide, including considerations to get started, steps to follow, sample content, and evaluation. You can use these models to help you create your own self-paced instruction. The video model plan can be used in any type library. The LibGuide lesson is designed for a public library but can be modified for yours.

Take a Video Tour of the Library

YOUTUBE

Figure 8.6. Syracuse University Libraries virtual tour.

Video Lesson

You can create videos for any number of topics—information literacy (e.g., creating a search strategy, the difference between scholarly journals and popular magazines), job-related topics (e.g., how to interview for a job or use Facebook), the library catalog, and many more. Videos lend themselves to different learning styles, and because they are self-paced, they can be reviewed many times.

Programs for creating videos range from free software (e.g., Vimeo and Movie Maker) to the professional software discussed earlier (e.g., Captivate and Camtasia). This video lesson models tasks to consider when creating your own video.

This lesson includes three phases of creating a video or screencast: preproduction, production, and postproduction. A scenario is based on a needs assessment conducted by a special library to determine what patrons need. Each phase contains steps necessary to complete the tasks.

Preproduction: Getting Started with Video

Preproduction forms the basis of the video. It is the most time-consuming phase. The instruction librarian will share ideas on what the video should contain and will assign responsibilities and tasks. It is also helpful for the librarian to share his or her vision for the video and develop expectations for each step.

Scenario

Many special, academic, and public libraries subscribe to a certain number of proprietary databases, such as ProQuest, Dialog, EBSCO, or Factiva. You have a number of limited-English-speaking colleagues who would benefit from having the documents they retrieve from a search translated into their native languages. You have decided to use ProQuest Dialog, a new search service from Dialog, because it enables translation of documents into thirteen languages.

You have described the ProQuest Dialog search service and provided patrons with some information to read. *Note:* You can use another search service with which you are familiar if it has a translation feature—simply follow the same steps modeled here. The concept and technique are similar when searching other search services.

Task

You will create a two- to three-minute self-paced video that demonstrates to your patrons, step-by-step, how to create a search strategy, conduct the search, and translate documents in ProQuest Dialog. You will conduct a medical search in one or more medical databases related to hypoglycemia as it affects the heart in women.

Step 1: Identify Goals and Objectives for the Video

Decide what you want your patrons to accomplish after watching the video. The goals and objectives are integral to assessment and provide the outcomes to evaluate:

Goals—At the end of the video, patrons will be able to translate search results into a different language.

Objectives—After viewing the video, patrons will be able to

- Conduct a search using advanced search in ProQuest Dialog
- View results
- Translate the records into a different language

Step 2: Review Materials

- Gather background material on ProQuest Dialog, including training and support aids about the system, at http://support.dialog.com/training/proquestdialog/.
- Review videos and search aids showing features and techniques of ProQuest Dialog so that you are very familiar with the search service before starting to create the video. At-a-glance screencasts, created with Captivate, are available at http://support.dialog.com/training/proquestdialog/#tabview=tab2, as are YouTube videos at http://www.youtube.com/playlist?list=PLBC0FC3A509EB66FC.

Step 3: Create a Storyboard and Script

- Ask yourself questions about the search: What topic will you choose that is appropriate for a proprietary database? How much of the search process will you show in the video? What database (or databases) will you search? What search terms will you use? What languages will you use for translation?

- Write your search on a worksheet (see figure 7.4). Select three or four search terms and write them in separate columns. Add synonyms to each column. Add wild-cards—for example, an asterisk (*) for unlimited number of letters, a question mark (?) to take the place of one letter—and select correct Boolean connectors.
- Map out your storyboard, identifying the progression of the search and any rein-forcement branching that will take place. Make sure that evaluation is part of the process (see handout 8.1).
- Try the search on ProQuest Dialog, review the results, and check one or more records to translate.
- Use the drop-down boxes to select the current language and the language that you want to translate the records into (see figure 8.7).
- Review the translation, then write a script explaining the process of the search in detail.
- Review, if possible, the script and storyboard with someone who is familiar with ProQuest Dialog.

Citation/Abstract « Back to results

☐ Add to selected items   🗐 Save to My Research ✉ Email 🖨 Print

Hypoglycemia and embryonic heart development

Smoak, Ida W 🗙; NLM. **Frontiers in bioscience : a journal and virtual library** 7 (Jan 1, 2002): d307-18. 💲 Pricing

Hide highlighting

Show duplicate items from other databases

⊟ **Abstract (summary)** Translate

| Abstract | ⊗ |
| From English ▼ | To Arabic ▼ |

Arabic
Chinese (Simplified)
Chinese (Traditional)
French
German
Italian
Japanese
Korean
Polish
Portuguese
Russian
Spanish
Turkish
cpp

Abnormal embryonic development is a comp   the most common and detrimental congenital malformations of the diabetic embryo common side effect of diabetes therapy and is a potential teratogen. An associ cemia and congenital defects has been difficult to demonstrate in humans, but in vivo dies have illustrated the importance of glucose as a substrate for normal development. H ryonic heart morphology, producing abnormal looping and chamber expansion, decre ss, disorganized layers, and decreased overall size. Hypoglycemia decreases embr vascularity, and it alters embryonic heart metabolism by increasing glucose up Hypoglycemia also affects protein expression in the embryonic heart, increasin cose regulated proteins, hexokinase, and glucose transport protein. Thus, hypoglyc mal cardiogenesis and alters morphology, function, metabolism, and expression of developing heart. It is likely that these factors contribute to heart defects observed in the diabetic embryopathy, but the definitive link has yet to be made. Future studies are expected to further elucidate mechanisms mediating hypoglycemia-induced cardiac dysmorphogenesis.

Figure 8.7. ProQuest Dialog screenshot.

HANDOUT 8.1. Sample Storyboard Template

Video Title: _____

Screen No.	Video	Audio	Duration
	Image: Add image here to represent video/still image that you will use—or write a description of it.	*Narration:* Write narration here to correspond with video (spoken and written text)	How long?
	Effects: Add notes describing effects or special shots (e.g., highlight boxes, shapes, zoom)	*Sound effects*: Add information about sound effects, music, or other audio	
	Transition: Add notes regarding how to transition from one screen clip to next?	*Transition:* Add notes regarding how to transition from one sound to next?	

Also during the production phase, the instruction librarian or the person who is most familiar with the video software will record the screencast. The librarian must review the video and audio recordings to make sure they are accurate and synchronized and to make any necessary changes.

Step 4: Create the Video Using Captivate

- Record a new demonstration project with Captivate. Following the storyboard, complete your search on ProQuest Dialog in advanced search while Captivate records all of your actions. *Note:* These instructions assume knowledge of Captivate or another video-creating software.
- Save your work and preview the video, rerecording any part that you are not satisfied with.
- Then, using Captivate or another audio program (e.g., Audacity), record your script so that the audio matches the actions that you see on the screen. Think of creating a PowerPoint slide show and adding audio to each slide. *Note:* You can also create PowerPoint slides and audio and insert the presentation into Captivate.

Step 5: Test and Revise the Video

- Preview the video in small chunks, editing where needed.
- Have someone who is unfamiliar with the topic and ProQuest Dialog try the video to see if anything is not clearly stated.

During postproduction, the rough video, audio, sequencing of images, and special effects must be processed. The final product must be compared with the storyboard to make sure that it contains all parts. An important piece is to make sure that the video tells the story that the librarian had as part of the original vision for the video. Evaluation should also occur.

Step 6: Putting It All Together

- Synchronize the audio and video, and add any highlight boxes or arrows, to point to parts of screens that you want to emphasize.
- Include background music, if desired.
- Add a learning check to assess whether patrons can create and conduct a search on ProQuest Dialog and translate the results into a different language.
- Have several librarians preview the video and make any final changes.
- Publish the video on the library website or on YouTube.

Step 7: Evaluate What Was Learned

- Have patrons try the video, and ask them to complete the survey about it, using handout 8.2.
- You could also create a short learning check as part of the video. You must create a branching scenario, where you plan to create the learning check first in the storyboard, to then transfer to your video. Incorporating practice of the tasks would also be helpful if it is not just a demonstration but a simulation.

- Complete a self-evaluation to evaluate the process that you went through to the completed video. This will help you decide what you like or dislike and what you might do differently for the next video (see handout 8.3; for additional resources, see table 8.3).

Table 8.3. URLs for Video Lesson

DESCRIPTION	URL
Jing free video software	http://www.techsmith.com/jing.html
Microsoft Photo Story 3 for Windows XP	http://www.microsoft.com/en-us/download/details.aspx?id=11132
Movie Maker	http://windows.microsoft.com/en-us/windows-live/movie-maker-get-started#t1=overview
iMovie for Apple	http://www.apple.com/ilife/imovie/
Videos for University of California at Berkeley	http://www.lib.berkeley.edu/Help/tutorials.php
Captivate tutorial on PDFs for articles via University of California–eLinks	http://www.lib.uci.edu/uc-research-tutorial/basic_19.html
Pubchem videos from Berkeley	http://www.lib.berkeley.edu/CHEM/instruction/pubchem/index.htm
How to use video editor for YouTube videos	http://support.google.com/youtube/bin/answer.py?hl=en&answer=183851
Tutorials and best practices for using Blackboard Collaborate	http://www.uis.edu/colrs/learning/technologies/elluminate/

ⓖ LibGuide Lesson: Integrating Modes of Instruction

Instruction librarians may be called on to deliver training to other librarians. This lesson plan combines different types of training that you have reviewed throughout this book, including face-to-face instruction, blended instruction, and self-paced asynchronous materials. The tasks demonstrate how you can integrate different types of training to make the most of this staff development learning opportunity. Two additional sessions will be conducted online, with the final session a face-to-face workshop.

Workshop Scenario

The instruction librarian has created a LibGuide for the state public library where she works. She has been asked to provide a workshop for other librarians in the area so that they too can create their own LibGuides for their public libraries. She is putting together a Basics LibGuide 101 blended self-development workshop. The first session will be face-to-face, to be held at the state library.

Attendees will create a group of LibGuides as the final product for the workshop. Participants will have a working product to use in their libraries. LibGuides by Springshare, used worldwide, is a versatile tool for any library. Academic libraries create course and research guides and use LibGuides as aids in library instruction. Public libraries create research portals, book club pages, and guides for job seekers, young readers, and

HANDOUT 8.2. Video Evaluation

Video Title: _____ *Date:* _____

Directions: Please rate the video according on the following quality indicators (1 = *poor*, 5 = *excellent*). Give comments where appropriate.

1. Was the content of the video accurate and up-to-date?
   1   2   3   4   5
   Comments: _____

2. Was the content of the video generally useful?
   1   2   3   4   5
   Comments: _____

3. Can you perform the tasks presented in the video?
   1   2   3   4   5
   Comments: _____

4. Were the objectives or key elements made clear in the introduction?
   1   2   3   4   5
   Comments: _____

5. Was the content detail controlled to promote understanding?
   1   2   3   4   5
   Comments: _____

6. Did the video try to cover too much material or introduce too much detail?
   1   2   3   4   5
   Comments: _____

7. Was practice of the skills presented built into the video?
   1   2   3   4   5
   Comments: _____

8. Did the video meet the learning objectives and your needs as a learner?

   1   2   3   4   5

   Comments: _____

9. Did what was visually depicted fit the learning objectives?

   1   2   3   4   5

   Comments: _____

10. Was the video well planned, organized, and structured?

    1   2   3   4   5

    Comments: _____

11. Overall, how would you rate the video?

    1   2   3   4   5

    Comments: _____

HANDOUT 8.3. Video Self-Evaluation Review Form

Video Title: _____

Reviewer's Name: _____ *Date:* _____

Directions: Review the video storyboard and completed video. For each characteristic, assign a value from 1 to 5 (1 = *strongly agree*, 2 = *agree*, 3 = *unsure*, 4 = *disagree*, 5 = *strongly disagree*).

Characteristic	Points
Readability is good (text, labels, numbers).	
Instructions are clear.	
Higher-level skills are taught whenever possible.	
Text is broken into appropriate steps/segments.	
Screens have enough "white space."	
Organized well and easy to follow.	
Formats are consistent (prompts, instructions, error messages, command inputs).	
Highlighting is consistent in its purpose.	
Response time is appropriately controlled.	
Target audience is clear.	
Graphics are legible, appropriately placed, and represent information.	
Links are made to prior knowledge.	
Learning options are plentiful in video.	
There is a high level of consistency in the design throughout the screens.	

Answer the following:

1. My favorite thing about the storyboard is

_____

2. I think the storyboard could be improved by

_____

3. I would do the following differently when I create my next video

_____

local teachers. Special libraries create customized research guides for their patrons, and all libraries can use them to market their libraries.

Workshop 1

As you begin your planning, integrate several important principles of adult learning: active participation, team learning, experience-based opportunities, and attention to learning styles and specific needs. Consider anxieties that learners may experience with this new type of online aid so that conducting pacing activities, providing adequate handouts to reinforce learning, and offering diverse ways to assess participants' learning are part of your planning.

Step 1: Preplanning the Workshop

A needs assessment indicates that librarians may be at various stages in their knowledge of LibGuides. You will need to identify these differences and plan for them.

Learning about LibGuides. Send an e-mail to librarians serviced by the state library, along with a colorful flyer announcing upcoming workshops on creating LibGuides. Indicate the purpose and goals of the workshops, including time, date, and place. List tasks that they should perform before the first session:

1. Look at several LibGuides from libraries similar to their own.
2. Review and comment on a "how to get started" video on LibGuides.
3. Write down several topics that they think will make effective LibGuides for their libraries.

Set up for the workshop. Have the room set up, ideally with work stations for all participants or, at minimum, so attendees can work in pairs. Make sure that drinks are available, create an agenda, and prepare all handouts and activities that you plan to present at the workshop. Make sure that the technology is operating correctly and that help is available if needed. Identify an assistant to help.

Step 2: Introduce the First Workshop—Ten Minutes

Introducing the workshop topic, yourself, and what attendees can expect is important to eliminate any anxieties they may have.

- Perform introductions, point out logistics, and review an agenda that not only includes the day's session but explains a bit about the online sessions to follow. Note that participants will have time during the workshop to acclimate themselves to what LibGuides are, why these workshops are needed, and how LibGuides will be advantageous to patrons in their libraries.
- Ask them how much they know about LibGuides and how much they are called on in their own libraries to work with and answer questions about technology and other topics.
- Review objectives for the workshop, indicating that attendees will participate in activities to familiarize themselves with LibGuides, their features, and well-developed examples.

Step 3: Begin the Warm-Up Exercise—Twenty Minutes

The warm-up exercise ensures that participants will understand what a LibGuide is and that they will get to know those attendees they have not met before.

- Ask participants to identify LibGuides that they particularly liked or disliked, why or why not, and, if possible, what they would have done differently if they had created one.
- Use the whiteboard to project some of the LibGuides so that all can review the sites together.
- Make a list of LibGuide characteristics.
- Ask attendees to introduce themselves to the person next to them and to ask questions that elicit facts about their partner, including his or her experience with technology, what he or she wants to take away from this workshop, and an idea for a LibGuide. Have them jot down the answers so that they can introduce their partner to the group.
- Have students introduce their colleague, and tell them that they will be working in pairs and groups during the workshop.

Step 4: Conduct Part 1 of the Workshop—Forty-Five Minutes

You will learn about the LibGuide and its features in part 1. Use one of the LibGuides reviewed during the warm-up to point out the different parts of a LibGuide.

- Review information from the warm-up by defining a LibGuide—that is, it can contain one or more pages on any topic, for any purpose, and it consists of pages (tabs), subpages (drop-down list from a tab), and boxes of content (text, links, RSS feeds, videos, polls, widgets, etc.).
- Show a public library LibGuide with a number of tabs. On the home page, point out the different boxes.
- Review figure 8.8 and have each pair of participants select a feature of a LibGuide. Each pair will demonstrate to the group how to set up the feature and show a page with this feature. Select one of the following: profile, boxes, links, RSS feeds, rich text, podcasts, videos, widgets, books from catalogs, polls and surveys, documents and files, Google boxes to add searches, and feedback boxes.
- Take a ten-minute break before presentations.
- After the break, have each pair present its feature to the whole group (thirty minutes)—specifically, demonstrate how to use the feature on a LibGuide template that the instructor has provided. Each pair can also find a video illustrating step-by-step instructions on its feature.
- This concludes the activities of the face-to-face introductory workshop. Explain the logistics for the two online sessions to follow in subsequent weeks.

Step 5: Follow-Up—Next Step; Ten Minutes

Follow-up is an important part of any training, especially when instructing on technology. It helps to reinforce the skills and concepts that participants learned in the workshop.

Figure 8.8. LibGuides help and documentation.

Recap the main points from the workshop, and indicate that attendees should complete the following before the first online session:

- Review the online system available to their libraries—in this lesson, the Blackboard learning management system. See chapter 7 for a refresher on using Blackboard.
- Alone or with someone else from their library, select a topic for a LibGuide that they would like to create (e.g., content topic, information literacy, employment, favorite books, special group such as seniors or teens).
- Have them start gathering content for the LibGuide. Create a graphic map outlining the structure of the guide they are proposing. Create a table of URLs and descriptions of the items to include, similar to the tables in this chapter.

Webinar 1

This one-hour session provides a cost-effective way for librarian attendees to meet with less time lost from their work and no travel cost. Before the session, the instructor will send out, by e-mail, information that attendees need to log on to Blackboard.

The instructor begins by reviewing a necessary few points for attendees to be able to navigate through Blackboard to complete the tasks for the webinar. This includes information on using the whiteboard and breakout rooms.

Step 1: Work through Activity 1—Twenty Minutes

The instructor conducts a quick demonstration on features in Blackboard that attendees will need for the following activities, then shows the agenda of tasks for the session. The instructor notes that activity 1 will help them organize their ideas on topics for their LibGuides.

- Introduce a poll showing possible topics for their LibGuides, and ask attendees to rank them in priority order. Show results on the whiteboard.
- Ask attendees to write the topics that they are considering for their LibGuides, using the whiteboard tools or in the chat. Review new topics not in the poll, especially those that had more than one person considering it.
- The instructor will quickly organize the responses into five numbered categories on the whiteboard. This visual map will form the basis of topics for individual LibGuides (see figure 8.9 as a model).
- Ask attendees to choose the category that they would like to work on by raising their hands using the webinar tools when the category is called.
- The instructor will assign members to groups 1–5 to breakout rooms based on attendees' votes and will load each category from the visual map onto a breakout room's whiteboard.

Step 2: Begin Activity 2 in Groups—Ten Minutes

The moderator has already set up five breakout rooms with whiteboards before the webinar. However, more rooms can be created as needed. Attendees can view one another in breakout rooms, if desired. The whiteboards will enable a high level of interactivity during the breakout sessions.

- Each group will name a leader and add to the category on the whiteboard possible types of content that they want to appear in their LibGuides.
- The instructor will moderate the breakout rooms as discussions ensue.

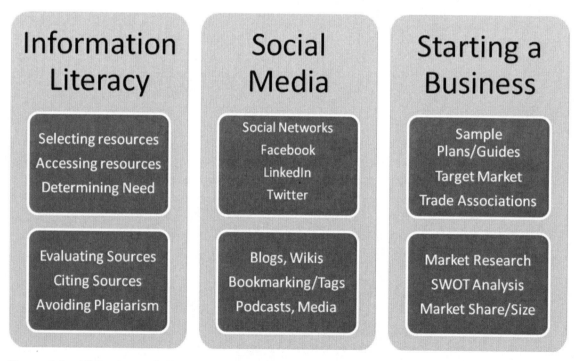

Figure 8.9. LibGuide visual maps.

- At the end of the group work, each group will save its whiteboard, and the moderator will copy all the whiteboards from the breakout rooms to the main room so that each group can discuss its ideas.

Step 3: Return to Main Room for Activity 3—Fifteen Minutes

- Have each group leader present the group's ideas for content for its LibGuide and any questions.
- The instructor comments on the group's ideas if necessary; other attendees can ask questions or provide comments in the chat that the group or the instructor can answer.

Step 4: Present Demonstration—Ten Minutes

- The instructor will provide a brief demonstration of how to use the LibGuide template and create a new template, if time allows.
- The instructor will describe the assignment: Each group should have created a template for its LibGuide and started writing any text, URLs for videos, and other materials to populate the LibGuide.

Step 5: Wrap Up the Webinar—Five Minutes

The instructor concludes with instructions for the webinar the following week:

- Have all materials that they plan to include in their LibGuides ready to input into the template.
- Indicate that the next session will be mostly a working session in their groups.

Webinar 2

Webinar 2 is a hands-on online workshop where groups can work on their LibGuide projects. Each group will use a breakout room to craft its template, including setting up tabs for each section of the LibGuide. Groups should have collected and written text for their guides prior to this online session.

Step 1: Start Creating the LibGuide—Thirty Minutes

Groups will do the following:

- Work together to design and approve the template.
- On the whiteboard, make changes where necessary to the map of the LibGuide parts, which they created from the previous assignment.
- Select the parts of the LibGuide that they will be in charge of, and lay out the boxes on the whiteboard. Using application sharing in Blackboard, have each person enter data into his or her LibGuide box.
- Complete a draft of the LibGuide for review.
- Review the content, make revisions where needed, and save.
- Note that the instructor will be monitoring the breakout rooms during this work session.

Step 2: Review LibGuide as a Whole Class—Twenty-Five Minutes

- Each group will have five minutes to present the draft of its LibGuide to the class.
- Other attendees will make suggestions and comments in the chat. One group member will monitor the chat and take notes.

Step 3: Wrap Up the Webinar—Five Minutes

The instructor will make final comments on the draft LibGuides, noting that the final versions should be sent to the instructor by midweek so that they can be distributed and reviewed by the entire class.

It is important to use the face-to-face session for discussion, interaction, and analysis. Therefore, having the LibGuides due before the last face-to-face workshop provides more time for discussion.

Workshop 2

Step 1: Review Final Project—Forty Minutes

- All groups will place their final LibGuides online using the channel used to communicate throughout the session. The other groups will review and critique the LibGuides to prepare for class discussion (see handout 8.4).
- Face-to-face, each group will discuss what went well in the project, what problems they had, what they liked or disliked about the group work, and how they felt about the blended instruction.
- Using the critiques that they completed before the session, groups will comment on each LibGuide, identifying positive aspects and changes they think are needed and why.
- Groups will make changes to their LibGuides based on those discussed.
- The instructor will demonstrate publishing a LibGuide to their library site. Each group will be responsible for publishing its own guide.

Step 2: Evaluate What Was Learned

Each attendee completes a staff development evaluation form (use handout 8.5). The instructor should also complete a checklist assessing the group of sessions—what went well, how the groups handled the learning management system technology, where there were misunderstandings, how the groups interacted, and whether the final LibGuides met expectations. This information will be useful for other instruction librarians presenting a blended course and for those who will be creating LibGuides on their own. See table 8.4 for more resources.

HANDOUT 8.4. Group Critique Form

Group: _____ Date: _____

Names of people in the group:

_____   _____

_____   _____

List the steps you followed in planning and completing your project.

_____

_____

_____

List the contributions made by each member of the group.

Name   Contribution

_____   _____

_____   _____

_____   _____

_____   _____

Identify any problems the group had and how the group resolved its problems.

_____

_____

_____

What changes would you make if you were to lead this type of project?

_____

_____

What did you learn from this project?

_____

_____

What was the best/worst thing about working in small groups in a blended learning environment?

_____

_____

HANDOUT 8.5. Staff Development Evaluation Form

Event Title: _____ *Date:* _____

Please check yes/no to answer the following questions:

1. Was the message/topic relevant to your work environment?
    ☐ Yes
    ☐ No

2. Was the instructor able to communicate information/topic clearly?
    ☐ Yes
    ☐ No

3. Was the instructor well versed in using the technology?
    ☐ Yes
    ☐ No

4. Was the workshop well organized?
    ☐ Yes
    ☐ No

5. Were activities diverse enough to keep your attention and motivate you to learn?
    ☐ Yes
    ☐ No

6. Was your confidence in working with LibGuides increased as a result of this workshop?
    ☐ Yes
    ☐ No

7. Was your confidence in learning in a blended course increased as a result of this workshop?
    ☐ Yes
    ☐ No

8. Would you like additional one-on-one training in this subject?
    ☐ Yes
    ☐ No

Please comment on the following:

1. What part of the course was the most enjoyable or helpful to you?

    _____

    _____

2. What part did you like least?

    _____

    _____

3. Please list the most important thing that you learned as a result of the sessions.

    _____

    _____

4. What could have improved your experience in the sessions?

    _____

    _____

5. What other subjects would you like to cover in future in-services?

    _____

    _____

Table 8.4. URLs for Integrated LibGuide Lesson

DESCRIPTION	URL
Embed video	http://libguides.agnesscott.edu/content.php?pid=259236&sid=2147528
Embedding videos and playlists from YouTube	http://support.google.com/youtube/bin/answer.py?hl=en&answer=171780
Finding embeddable code on YouTube	http://libguides.agnesscott.edu/content.php?pid=259236&sid=2147528
Setting up breakout rooms in Blackboard	http://www.youtube.com/watch?v=2DlZJfHUAh4
Blackboard Guide including information on breakout rooms	http://www.uccs.edu/Documents/frc/Blackboard%20Blurbs/Collaborate%20WC/Collab_Engagement_TipsWP-final.pdf
Whiteboard tutorial for Blackboard	http://www.niu.edu/blackboard/tutorials/bbcollabwhiteboard.shtml
Tutorials and best practices for using Blackboard Collaborate	http://www.uis.edu/colrs/learning/technologies/elluminate
LibGuide template	http://research.wou.edu/clip

⊚ Key Points

Whether self-directed materials are technology (e.g., videos, screencasts, or tutorials), a web tool (e.g., Pinterest), or printed search aids (e.g., quick reference cards, maps to tour the library), they are becoming an integral part of the librarian's instructional toolbox. They are being used in combination with online and face-to-face instruction to reinforce learning. With the wide range of sophisticated but easy-to-use technology, librarians can often provide a learning environment that enhances instruction.

EXERCISES: Now You Try It . . .

To reinforce what you learned in this chapter, complete the following exercises.

1. Identify a task in your library that would benefit from a printed resource or could be created into a PDF document (e.g., a quick reference card, handout, short guide). Make sure it has the following:
   a. Title for resource
   b. Purpose—what user will achieve from using this resource
   c. Content that supports the purpose (e.g., how-to in form of steps)
   d. Visuals and branding of the library
   e. Pleasing, readable format
2. Depending on your library, create a LibGuide for a specific subject with a description of content for at least four tabs. If you do not have access to the LibGuide program, create a video or print handout.
3. Select at least five videos that you think will help teach your patrons about information literacy (e.g., selecting search terms, evaluating a website).

4. Review several Pinterest sites and select ones that you would like to pin on a site at your library. Sign up for your own Pinterest account and include some of the pins on your board. Pin some of the videos for teaching information literacy to your board.

5. Select a self-paced course or tutorial that you would like to introduce into your library. Create an outline stating objectives, describing what the resource will teach and how, and adding an evaluation component. Create a storyboard that would enable someone else to create your course. Explain what you think the advantages of this type of resource are for your subject.

6. View good examples of online learning materials. Remember to click on icons to view as many parts of courses as you possibly can. As you survey the materials, try to identify some unique characteristics or key features of the materials that are common to all the samples that you might incorporate into your library resources.

References

Bailey, R., G. Blunt, and M. Magner. 2011. "Librarian and Faculty Collaboration on Video Projects." *Kentucky Libraries* 75 (1): 16–18.

Experian Hitwise. 2012. "Instagram and Pinterest the New Global Stars of Social." http://www.experian.com/blogs/hitwise-uk/2012/08/22/instagram-and-pinterest-the-new-global-stars-of-social/.

Further Reading

Aslanian, C. B., and D. L. Clinefelter. 2012. *Online College Students 2012: Comprehensive Data on Demands and Preferences.* Louisville, KY: Learning House. http://www.learninghouse.com/files/documents/resources/Online%20College%20Students%202012.pdf.

Dick, Walter, Lou Carey, and James O. Carey. 2005. *The Systematic Design of Instruction.* 6th ed. New York: Pearson Education.

Lindsay, Elizabeth Blakesley. 2004. "The Best of Both Worlds: Teaching a Hybrid Course." *Academic Exchange Quarterly.* Washington State University. https://research.wsulibs.wsu.edu:8443/xmlui/handle/2376/746.

Lindsay, Elizabeth Blakesley, Lara Ursin Cummings, and B. Jane Scales. 2007. "Integrating Information Literacy into Distance Education: The Progression of an Online Course." *Research Exchange.* Washington State University. https://research.wsulibs.wsu.edu:8443/xmlui/handle/2376/1338.

Mayer, Richard E., and Ruth C. Clark. 2002. *E-Learning and the Science of Instruction: Proven Guidelines for Consumers and Designers of Multimedia Learning.* New York: Wiley.

O'Donnell, R. E., N. Pomea, J. Rawson, R. Shepard, and C. Thomes. 2010. "Library-Led Faculty Workshops: Helping Distance Educators Meet Information Literacy Goals in the Online Classroom." *Journal of Library Administration* 50 (7/8): 830–56. http://www.inthelibrarywiththeleadpipe.org/2009/sense-of-self-embracing-your-teacher-identity/.

Rummel, Jennifer. 2012. "How to Use Pinterest for Your Library." *Voya* (June). https://pinterest/com/yabooknerd?d.

CHAPTER 9

What's Ahead for the Instruction Librarian?

Information literate people are those who have learned how to learn. They know how to find information, and how to use information in such a way that others can learn from them. They are people prepared for lifelong learning because they can always find the information needed for any task or decision at hand.

—AMERICAN LIBRARY ASSOCIATION PRESIDENTIAL COMMITTEE

ON INFORMATION LITERACY (January 10, 1989)

What to Expect

The academic library in the information age will be a teaching library, and educating students in the information literacy skills of identifying, locating, accessing, and evaluating information has become a fundamental responsibility for academic librarians. Public libraries also provide instruction every day—whether for a patron filling out an online job application or using resources to pass a job certification exam, a grandmother learning to e-mail her grandson overseas, or a student studying for college exams. Information professionals in special libraries describe examples that are highly relevant to their patrons in training sessions, such as detailed searches on the subjects of greatest interest to the participants.

Many instruction librarians also develop customized, downloadable, written materials. However, all librarians must continue to learn—not only about new information retrieval, distribution and collaboration tools, and communication technologies but also about subjects that they may not have encountered in their library training, including teaching strategy, curriculum development, instructional design, adult learning, and strategic marketing.

The core competencies of information literacy center on identifying an information need; accessing needed information; evaluating, managing, and applying information; and understanding the legal, social, and ethical aspects of information use. Teaching those abilities is the role of the library—whether public, academic, or special. The systematic delivery of such instructional programs and services should be planned in concert with overall strategic library planning.

As part of this educational goal, instruction librarians need to keep pace with innovations in educational technology that provide ways of efficiently and effectively storing and delivering their instructional messages. It is not the technology itself that affects learning; rather, educational technology can facilitate the teaching and learning process. It has the potential to make education richer and more stimulating by creating environments and presenting content not possible otherwise. Understanding the learner and the process of organizing instruction are the critical issues of educational technology. Accommodating the individual by tailoring instruction to his or her needs and discovering the most effective means of using technology to facilitate learning are the important concerns.

Online learning has yet to reach its full potential. When instruction librarians become fully acclimated to teaching and using technology and when academic faculty accept them as full partners in the teaching process, librarians will continue to increase their value to learning. Moreover, as more public libraries become hubs of the community and partner with other learning organizations, the amount of online training in the public library will continue to increase. Businesses in particular are looking for learning solutions that deliver the right educational experiences at the moment they are needed, in the most useful format, and in the most economical manner. Current trends will continue to help this happen.

More Social Interaction

The encroachment of social tools into people's lives is deepening every day and changing the way that people relate to one another, exchange ideas, and interact with organizations. The ease with which individuals can share through social tools makes them more likely to do so; in an instructional setting, this might start to translate into increased peer-to-peer learning.

More Mobile Tools

Apple released the first iPad in January 2010. While the digital world was already becoming more mobile with each new hardware release, the introduction of tablet computers fundamentally changed the place of mobile content in professional, educational, and personal lives. Smart phones, a wider range of tablet devices, e-readers and e-books, and further development of resources specifically designed to be used via mobile devices are continuing this evolution. Instruction librarians must be aware of mobile-enabled tools as a means to deliver instruction and accommodate students who ask for such versions of online learning programs.

More Ease of Use

Tools are becoming more user-friendly with every iteration. Next-generation tools become ever more intuitive and continue the trend toward graphic-driven interfaces that look and feel similar to software and systems that users are already familiar with.

As instruction librarians gain more experience with learning theory, instructional design, and teaching, the learning curve will no longer be overwhelming. They will be adapting existing knowledge rather than engaging with an entirely new process. At the same time, the youngest generation of adults participating in online learning will have a greater presence in more classrooms. This generation is extremely tech savvy and quite comfortable experimenting with tools to get them to work. As more and more members of this generation show up for educational opportunities, they will push their instructors to explore even more potential directions for their learning experiences. Instruction librarians must be ready for the challenge.

Today, library use and the number of adults with library cards are increasing, not decreasing, as libraries have embraced technology and the Internet. Libraries have websites and are reaching out to patrons outside their physical buildings. By providing a more diverse collection of information, new technology (e.g., e-books, downloadable audio books), technology training, and educational and recreational gaming, libraries are working to meet the greater demands of their patrons.

⑥ Promote Library Services and Programs

In a tight economy and among funding cuts, marketing is playing an increasingly important role in the work of libraries. One of the most crucial marketing needs for libraries is to reach out to those who do not know the gamut of services provided by their institutions. When it comes to seeing the value in libraries and their resources, librarians need to leverage a mode of teaching that allows patrons to experience all that the library has to offer. However, as with teaching methodology, marketing is not one of the skills frequently taught in library school.

Many effective marketing techniques exist for providing awareness of library programs such as information literacy. Fliers, bookmarks, and library instruction handouts will help market the online information literacy services, but these reach only students and patrons who visit the library. Instruction librarians must be more creative to reach students outside the library walls to make patrons aware of what they have. Patron comments indicate a lack of knowledge about online tools, such as databases, e-books, and online training. To ensure that new tutorials or videos are used and to maximize usage of current offerings, librarians need to put additional energy into informing patrons of the wealth of online tools offered by the library.

Social networking services (e.g., Facebook, Twitter, blogs, Google+) are used to publicize library events, such as gaming nights; to alert users to additions to collections; to provide links to articles, videos, or web content that might prove relevant or helpful to patrons; and to provide a conduit for community information. Social media also plays an important role in fostering relationships with the community by allowing patrons to ask questions or provide feedback about library services. When a library's Facebook followers share the library's content, they are acting as a type of advocate for the library by helping spread its message.

Pinterest is also a way to promote events at the public library, connect with students in a class, or provide graphics of topics that you want to teach. For example, an instruction librarian in a public library may be planning a session on how to put together a resume for patrons who are looking for jobs. A "Create a Pinterest Resume" image may be helpful as a handout, or it may appear on the library's website. A YouTube video pinned by the University of Texas demonstrates how to use Pinterest to collect open education resources. An infographic illustrates using e-books, a topic that patrons want to know more about. These are but a few teaching resources drawn together on one Pinterest board.

Patrons of all kinds must embrace the concept of the library as a virtual learning community. The instruction librarian in a public library can communicate the value of the library as an essential support system for economic recovery by participating actively in the community and using these experiences to inform and deepen interactions with patrons. By tracking metrics over time, the librarian can measure outcomes of services and programs for the unemployed. Collecting and broadcasting stories and anecdotes about patrons' successful acquisition of twenty-first-century skills and concepts announces and promotes achievement. Providing a current and relevant collection of online and print materials helps the economically affected grasp the changing demands of the workforce. These resources also increase users' awareness and understanding of the impact of globalization on the workforce. Finally, instruction librarians can provide guidance to support new users' effective use of online and digital resources so that library patrons in public, academic, and special libraries will have the tools they need for twenty-first-century jobs.

Reference

American Library Association Presidential Committee on Information Literacy. 1989. *A Progress Report on Information Literacy: An Update on the American Library Association Presidential Committee on Information Literacy: Final Report, March 1998*. Washington, DC: American Library Association. http://www.ala.org/acrl/publications/whitepapers/presidential.

Further Reading

American Library Association. 2009. *Libraries Connect Communities 3: Public Library Funding and Technology Access Study*. Chicago: American Library Association. http://www.ala.org/plinternetfunding.

Association of College and Research Libraries. 2011. "Guidelines for Instruction Programs in Academic Libraries." Revised. http://www.ala.org/acrl/standards/guidelinesinstruction.

Rogers, Curtis R. 2011. *Social Media, Libraries and Web 2.0: How American Libraries Are Using New Tools for Public Relations and to Attract New Users—Fourth Annual Survey*. South Carolina State Library. http://www.statelibrary.sc.gov/docs/pr/201202_com_social_media_survey_dec_2011.pdf.

Index

active learning. *See* learning

ADDIE Model, 16–17, 111. *See also* instructional design

Adobe Acrobat Connect Pro, 123

Adobe Captivate. *See* Captivate

ARCS Model, 15–16. *See also* instructional design

assessment. *See* evaluation

asynchronous, 60, 97, 101–2, 137; creating, 107–11; examples, 106–7; *See also* e-learning

behaviorism, 3–4

Bell, Steven. *See* blended learning

bias, 79. *See also* evaluation, websites

Blackboard, 119–22, 125–26, 161, 168

blended learning, 16, 97, 102–3, 124. *See also* e-learning

blogs, 85. *See also* social media evaluation

Bloom, Benjamin. *See* Bloom's Taxonomy

Bloom's Taxonomy, 16–18, 107

Boolean connectors, 131, 138, 152

Brunner, Jerome. *See* constructivism

Camtasia, 107, 141–42, 150

Captivate, 140, 142, 150–51, 154

cognitivism, 3–5

communication skills, 35–36

constructivism, 3, 5

copyright, 125–27

deductive learning. *See* instruction

Dialog, xv, xvi, 129, 151

e-learning, 96; forms of, 96–97; strategies, 127. *See also* online learning; webinars

embedded librarian, 63, 103

Environment Protection Agency National Library Network, 14

evaluation, 21–22, 26, 127; action plan, 42–43; criteria, 71–74, 77–78; form, 44, 80; formative, 21, 40–41, 133; model, 43; self-evaluation, 26, 83, 86–87, 158; social media, 78–82; summative, 21, 81, 84, 133, 154, 156–58, 165–67; websites, 45

experiential learning. *See* learning

face-to-face training, 56–60, 67; classroom, 56–58; one-on-one, 59; presence, 68–69; small group, 59–60; visuals, 69; workshops, 58–59, 155

flipped classroom, 102, 139

Gagne, Robert. *See* Gagne's Nine Events of Instruction

Gagne's Nine Events of Instruction, 18–21

Gardner, Howard. *See* learning styles; multiple intelligences

goals. *See* lesson, goals

graphic organizer, 19, 24, 40–41. *See also* visual maps

handouts, 42, 69–70

humanist, 3, 5

independent learning, 55

indirect instruction. *See* self-paced courses

inductive. *See* instruction

information literacy, 71

information professional, xix

information search process, model of, 7

information sources, 24. *See also* lesson plans

Institute of Museum and Library Services, 95

instruction: best practices, 33–34; characteristics, 32–33; delivery, 33, 50, 56; design, 37; online, 60–61; sources of, 62–63; strategies, 52–55, 57, 70; techniques, 35, 45; types, 50, 53; skills, 34–36

instructional design, 15, 27, 34–35; components, 18

Jing, 140, 142

Keller, J. M. *See* instructional design

Kirkpatrick, D. L., 43

Knowles, Malcolm, 3, 6

Kolb, David, 3, 5, 8–10. *See also* learning; learning styles

Kuhlthau, Carol. *See* learning, theories

learners: active involvement, 41; individual differences, 38

learning, 3–4; active, 45, 57; characteristics of, 4; children, 4; experiential cycle of, 5–6; independent, 55; inquiry-based, 55; structure, 42; theories, 3–6, 10

learning management system, 119–21, 123, 125

learning styles, 3, 8–10

lesson: goals, 40, 75, 85, 125, 129, 151; LibGuide, 155, 159–68; planning, 36, 38; video lesson, 150–58

lesson plan model: evaluating websites, 75–85; small group instruction in the public library, 85–91

lesson plans, 46; Gagne's Events of Instruction, 21–26, 28; template, 47

LibGuides, 143–44; examples, 145–46; workshop, 155, 159–68

LMS. *See* learning management system

marketing, 173–74

Merrill's principles, 8, 51–52

mobile tools, 172

Moodle, 119–20, 123. *See also* learning management system

multiple intelligences, 8–10. *See also* learning styles

needs assessment, 20, 75, 159. *See also* evaluation

objectives: chapter, 1, 13, 31, 49, 67, 95, 115, 137; lesson, 75, 85, 125, 130, 151; writing, 39–40

online learning, 95; advantages, 97–99; challenges, 99–100; tips, 123; virtual lesson, 124–27

open source LSM. *See* learning management system

outsourcing, 62–63

Piaget, Jean. *See* cognitivism

Pinterest, 143, 146–47, 173–74; examples, 148–49

ProQuest Dialog, 129, 131–34, 151–52

presentation skills, 35–36

Rogers, Carl. *See* humanist

rubric, 91, 128–29, 133–34. *See also* evaluation

SCORM, 142

search: strategies, 131; worksheet, 130–32

self-directed learning. *See* online learning

self-paced courses, 60–61

self-paced materials, 138–39, 143. *See also* online learning

Skinner, B. F. *See* behaviorism

social media evaluation, 78

storyboard. *See* videos

synchronous instruction, 60, 97, 101–2, 115; designing, 104–6; examples of, 103–4

teacher-centered instruction, 52. *See also* synchronous instruction

Tegrity, 123

Thorndike, Edward. *See* behaviorism

Toffler, Alvin, 1

videos, 139–40; advantages, 140–41; as teaching tool, 141; creating, 141–43, 150; disadvantages, 141; lesson plan, 150–58; library tour, 149–50; storyboard, 110, 141–43, 151, 153

virtual classroom. *See* online learning

visual maps, 162

VOIP, 97, 122

web-based training. *See* online learning

webinars, 97; characteristics, 116–17; webex, 119–20, 122–23, 131, 161–65. *See also* learning management system; online learning

YouTube, 140, 143–44, 168

About the Author

Beverley E. Crane received a bachelor of arts in curriculum and instruction, with a dual major in Spanish and English, and a master of education in bilingual education and English as a second language from Penn State University. She obtained a doctorate of education in curriculum and instruction, with emphases in language arts and educational technology, from Oklahoma State University. She has taught English/language arts and English as a second language at the middle school, high school, and college levels.

While working on a grant for a five-state multicultural resource center, she conducted workshops for teachers and librarians on such topics as literacy, writing, English as a second language, and integrating technology into the curriculum. For the last twenty-four years, she has also worked for Dialog, now a business of ProQuest, where she has created educational materials and conducted workshops and online training, teaching academic, public, and special librarians about online searching. She has presented at conferences throughout the United States—including those of the American Association of School Librarians, the International Society of Technology Educators, the American Educational Research Association, and the California Media and Library Educators Association, among others—on such topics as using online searching in the curriculum, computers and writing, and online research across the curriculum.

As director of the English education program at San Jose State University for five years, she has worked closely with classroom teachers, administrators, and librarians to provide guidelines for mentor teachers who supervise English student teachers. Currently, she continues to create training materials for Dialog, including distance education online courses and self-paced modules and videos on searching techniques, and she is editor of Dialog customer e-newsletters. Her books include *Teaching with the Internet: Strategies and Models for K–12 Curricula* (2000), *Internet Workshops: 10 Ready-to-Go Workshops for K–12 Educators* (2003), *Using Web 2.0 Tools in the K–12 Classroom* (2009), and *Using Web 2.0 Tools and Social Networking in the K–12 Classroom* (2012). She lives in Santa Fe, New Mexico, where she is involved with local art associations and continues to maintain a presence in the educational community.